Books in Craig Hickman's Management Game Series

The Strategy Game
The Organization Game
The Productivity Game

THE PRODUCTIVITY GAME

**An Interactive Business Game
Where YOU Make
or Break the Company**

CRAIG R. HICKMAN

PRENTICE HALL
Englewood Cliffs, New Jersey 07632

Prentice Hall International (UK) Limited, *London*
Prentice Hall of Australia Pty. Limited, *Sydney*
Prentice Hall Canada, Inc., *Toronto*
Prentice Hall Hispanoamericana, S.A., *Mexico*
Prentice Hall of India Private Limited, *New Delhi*
Prentice Hall of Japan, Inc., *Tokyo*
Simon & Schuster Asia Pte. Ltd., *Singapore*
Editora Prentice Hall do Brasil, Ltda., *Rio de Janeiro*

10 9 8 7 6 5 4 3 2 1

Library of Congress Cataloging-in-Publication Data

Hickman, Craig R.
    The productivity game / by Craig R. Hickman
        p.   cm.
    Includes bibliographical references.
    ISBN 0-13-158494-4
    1. Industrial productivity. 2. Management games. I. Title.
HD56.H53   1995
658.4'0353—dc20   95-5645
                                                                   CIP

If you would like to receive information about other products in Craig Hickman's
Management Game Series, please call 801-224-6661 or write to The Management Game
Series, P.O. box 50148, Provo, Utah 84605-0148

ISBN 0-13-158494-4

PRENTICE HALL
Career & Personal Development
Englewood Cliffs, NJ 07632

Simon & Schuster, A Paramount Communications Company

Printed in the United States of America

Dedication

To Phil Matthews, Tom Mullaney, Gary Coughlin, Brian McKinley, Bob Kidder, and Jim Scarborough who initiated my own consciousness of human productivity.

Preface

Many people helped me create this game, including Michael Snell, my literary agent and collaborator; Mary Kowalczyk and her associates at Word Masters who typed and revised the manuscript; Karen Hansen, senior editor at Prentice Hall; Pam Hickman, my wife and adviser; and numerous other family members, friends, clients, and associates who have contributed to the development of this game in countless ways.

The Productivity Game is the third in a series of business books (*The Strategy Game* and *The Organization Game* preceded it) intended to entertain readers by engaging them in a suspenseful exploration of the many avenues for increasing productivity and to stimulate learning by exposing readers to a broad range of productivity improvement ideas and concepts that can inform thinking and decision making for the new economy.

In the era of new management, people everywhere in an organization are expected to assume responsibility for overall results. To do so successfully, they must become more conscious of and competent in productivity improvement. *The Productivity Game* is designed to strengthen and test such consciousness and competence.

Before you begin playing *The Productivity Game*, I would like to offer advice similar to that provided in *The Strategy Game* and *The Organization Game*. You are being asked to make productivity decisions that will shape the future of fictitious FaraCom. The choices you face are intended to simulate real life; however, you may occasionally be presented with choices you consider to be extreme, inflexible, or contrived. Remember, this is a game that focuses on productivity-related decisions. I suggest that you consider any such circumstances as mere constraints, not unlike many similar circumstances and conditions that compose the world of today's CEOs. You may also feel that a lack of sufficient information or a narrow focus on productivity makes it impossible to make the best decision. As this occurs all too often in real life, use what you do know to stretch your thinking and make the best decision. Keep in mind that the mediocre and negative outcomes you encounter in the game are designed to stimulate your thinking and test your decision making. You may be able to make those choices that turn out mediocre or negative in the game successful and productive in real life. However, if you read the other alternatives available to you at each of the decision points, you will discover why the author considered one or more of the other alternatives a better choice. You are now ready to begin your productivity improvement experience at FaraCom.

I hope you find this book enjoyable and useful.

Craig R. Hickman

Contents

Contents

CHAPTER 1

Current Situation

For 12 years you built a lucrative career as a partner at Ernst & Young, a Big-6 accounting and consulting firm. Three months ago, when you finished facilitating a three-day strategy retreat for 24 top executives of the Faragut Communications and Entertainment Company, the founder and major stockholder of the company, William C. Faragut, invited you to dinner and asked you, in his customary blunt fashion, "What would it take for you to quit fiddling with companies from the outside and come inside where you can really get your hands dirty?" Though Faragut's words shocked you at first, they also challenged you to rethink your career in business strategy consulting, and after three months of courtship, you accepted the position as CEO of the Faragut Communications and Entertainment Company (FaraCom). Now, having finished your first day on the job, Bill Faragut's words of that fateful dinner come back to haunt you: Problems that appeared so simple from the outside look a lot different on the inside.

During your initial consulting engagement, you could clearly see major productivity problems in each of FaraCom's seven major divisions: book publishing; software and CD-ROM publishing; film and video production; cable television operations; catalogue sales and direct marketing; and retail operations. Now that those problems have fallen into your lap, however, they seem much more complex. Bill Faragut ran the company for the last ten years as a visionary opportunist, addressing productivity problems on a piecemeal basis. Now, recognizing the need for a strong CEO to

1

solve those problems in a deliberate, coordinated fashion and bring FaraCom into sustainable profitability, he has given you free rein to do just that. FaraCom has invested a lot of money in process mapping, reengineering, whole system design, and reorganization over the last two years, drawing upon some of the best consultants in the country. Unfortunately, the company can't seem to make the redesigned systems and revamped structure pay off in terms of individual and collective productivity.

You see great potential in the organization, which boasts combined divisional revenues of just over $500 million, but it has not realized that potential because low productivity throughout its divisions has eroded profitability for three years running. More than anything else, the concern of other shareholders pressured Bill Faragut to bring in a new CEO.

The following five-year summary of FaraCom operations tells the story:

Selected Financial and Productivity Information
(Revenues and Profits in $ Millions)

	Current Year	Previous Years			
Revenues	$508	$453	$391	$276	$188
Profits	($22)	($10)	$2	$18	$12
Employees	1,612	1,284	1,002	674	462
Revenues per Employee (Actual $)	$315,136	$352,804	$390,220	$404,496	$406,926
Profits per Employee (Actual $)	($13,648)	($7,788)	$1,996	$26,706	$25,974

You know Bill Faragut likes you but you also know he's a man of action who expects quick results, and you feel him looking over your shoulder every minute of your first day at the helm. It's a tough spot. You've put your whole career on the line in a situation that can make or break your reputation as a hands-on leader, and where your every decision will come under a microscope. Yet the stakes convinced you to take the risk: If you solve FaraCom's productivity problems quickly and well, you could gain up to 10 percent stock ownership of the company and begin realizing FaraCom's vast potential. On the other hand, if you fail to improve the company's productivity, you could ruin your career and extinguish FaraCom's potential.

Given the astonishing rate of change in the communications and entertainment industry, you know that each of FaraCom's divisions must become much more productive. Otherwise, the company will never be able to take advantage of all the opportunities that will spring up along the "information superhighway." As a first step in that direction you decide to evaluate the competence and commitment of Faragut's division presidents. The following diagram identifies those key people and shows the current revenues/profits of their respective divisions:

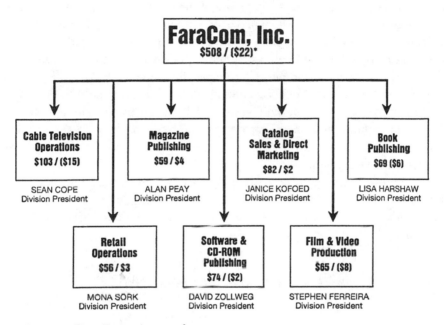

*Dollars in millions/Losses in parentheses

Your earlier consulting assignment with FaraCom dealt with the strategic and operational requirements attending the company's shift from telephony (i.e., television and telephone products and services) to computers and telecomputing devices (i.e., PCs with fax, modem, and CD-ROM capabilities). Three months ago you had urged FaraCom's executives to remain nimble and flexible, as well as systematic and efficient. That advice had gotten Bill Faragut's attention and prompted his pursuit of your skills.

With the information superhighway well on its way to fulfillment through the expanding Internet, and with condensed satellite dishes and fiber-optic cable spreading throughout the country, FaraCom must invent a brand new future because the future will not look anything like the past. The outcome of the battle for the future will, you now realize, hinge not only on nimbleness, flexibility, and an efficient, systematic effort, but on world-class productivity in every business FaraCom decides to enter.

After your first two weeks on the job as FaraCom's new CEO, you commute to your newly purchased home wondering where to place your initial focus. Should you focus on thinking about your own productivity as CEO of this company, primarily worrying about how to deploy your own effort over the next several months? Should you focus on the productivity of each of the seven division presidents, some of whom have worked for FaraCom since the beginning, some of whom have only recently joined the company? According to Bill Faragut, each of the division presidents needs training, development, and a lot of help from above. In fact, Bill has encouraged you to focus your time and attention here more than anywhere else. While that makes a certain amount of sense, you also consider the benefit of developing a companywide productivity system that can get the job done from the bottom up rather than from the top down. Which approach could achieve the greatest improvements in the shortest period of time? Which will produce the longest lasting benefits?

Settling into your office at home, you set these nagging questions aside for a moment and ponder, instead, everything you've learned over the years about productivity. During the next several hours you summarize the latest thinking on the subject.

SUMMARY OF THE LATEST THINKING ON PRODUCTIVITY

Jack Welch, chairman and CEO of General Electric, has frequently attributed the transformation at GE to a fundamental focus on increasing productivity. Given GE's remarkable success, numerous individuals and firms across the country have returned to researching and debating the topic as a possible means of simplifying and integrating all the proliferating management fads, techniques, and programs that have sprung up in recent years. Your own library contains a number of articles and books on the subject.

According to a special *Fortune* magazine "new economy" report, for example, computers, faxes, networks, the Internet, and other information technology tools have begun influencing national productivity statistics: nonfarm business productivity reached a 5 percent annual rate in the early 1990s, up from 1 percent in the 1980s. Manufacturing productivity grew 4 percent annually during the first half of this decade, up from an average of 2 percent in the 1980s. Productivity in the service industries has grown at a 2 percent annual rate in the 1990s, after falling in the 1970s and remaining flat in the 1980s. America continues to stay ahead of Japan and Europe in terms of productivity, but can America rack up 20 consecutive years of 5 percent or higher productivity gains? Not if current productivity methods end up merely promoting more mental stress, employee burnout, strained relationships, and family and social dysfunction.

In her bestselling book *The Overworked American*, Harvard Business School lecturer Juliet Schor analyzes 20 years of labor statistics, from 1970 to 1990, and concludes that "the average employed person is now on the job an additional 163 hours,... the equivalent of an extra month a year." Her research shows that "hours have risen across a wide spectrum of Americans and in all income categories—low, middle, and high. The increase is common to a variety of family patterns—people with and without children, those who are married, and those who are not. And it has been general across industries and, most probably, occupations." However, Schor also points out that no evidence suggests that longer hours lead to higher productivity. In fact, longer hours may create the opposite effect, especially if they prevent weary people from doing their best thinking.

Based on a recent survey conducted and published by *American Demographics*, "higher proportions of Americans feel they are always in a hurry." The survey asked respondents whether they "always," "sometimes," or "almost never" feel rushed to do the things they have to do. In response, "32 percent of Americans between the ages of 18 and 64 report[ed] that they always feel rushed to do the things they have to do... up from 25 percent in 1965."

Among the ranks of American managers, the problem of overwork looms even larger. In a timely and provocative feature article in Fortune magazine entitled "Welcome to the Age of Overwork," author Anne Fisher points out, "The survivors of mergers, downsizings, and cost cutting are hard pressed to get a day off." She summarizes the situation this way: "Precise statistics on the hours logged by U.S. managers are elusive for the simple reason that nobody has ever really counted the time that salaried people put in. But anecdotal evidence and a raft of surveys strongly suggest that many white-collar Americans are approaching the Japanese tradition of 12-hour days and work-filled evenings." Surveys from organizations such as Priority Management, a Seattle-based consulting firm, and the American Management Association suggest that the majority of managers work an average of 50–70 hours per week. Almost all of those surveyed admitted to fretting about how to live a more balanced life, and only "a tiny minority"— one in 50—say they're successful at "juggling everything."

The *Fortune* article concludes: "The greatest cost to corporations of stressing out managers over long periods of time is also the most ineffable.

It's impossible to say how much better a company might be doing if its managers weren't quite so busy or quite so tired. How many bad decisions might be avoided? How many innovative ideas might never have a chance to bloom? Remember Archimedes, lolling in his bath. To an observer, had there been one, he might have seemed to be doing nothing. His thoughts, of course, led to the discovery of the principle of displacement, a cornerstone of physics. Would he have reached the same conclusions in a quick shower?"

Despite these warnings about the current productivity crisis, however, your review of the literature also reveals new hopes and expectations for the future. In his book *Maximizing Employee Productivity*, author Robert Sibson points out, "Much of what is 'output' in the future will be open-ended, and that also presents a greater opportunity for increasing employee productivity. Until recent years, the numerator of the productivity equation (output) was limited by how much could be sold and used. For example, the number of shoes you could produce was limited by the number of pairs of feet in the world. As we move into the third leg of our economy, which is mostly personal care, leisure, and entertainment businesses, the output is less limited or unlimited. Mental activities, such as learning, for example, have no limit that we now understand, and there are some who think that the average life expectancy may become as much as 200 years."

In another recent book, *Work and the Human Spirit*, authors John Scherer and Larry Shook argue that "the quality of work we do cannot be separated from the quality of 'self' we manage to create in our lives." This observation raises two important implications for organizations. First, "Organizations have a vested interest in nurturing the human spirit of the work force, since the state of workers' spirits has a direct bearing upon the quality of their work. And because leaders act as 'speed governors' on the rest of the organization, it will help businesses to have people at the top who are awakening their own spirits." And, second, "Work that injures the human spirit, even it it's profitable, isn't good work in the end; companies ought to change that work as quickly as possible, because the forces of the marketplace (or the forces of the universe or whatever you want to call it) tend to punish soul-killing labor out of existence anyway." According to Scherer and Shook, the companies that "start caring about the quality of the inner lives of those who serve their customers, and start acting on that concern, will inevitably transform the world at work." In addition, they encourage workers to "find new purpose, engage deeply with your work, relate to people.... These are becoming the new prescriptions for how to succeed in business."

In yet another recent book, *Productive Workplaces*, author Marvin Weisbord explains that "productive workplaces are those where people learn and grow as they cooperate to improve an organization's performance. The 'bottom line,' in this way of looking at things, is dignity, meaning, and community in work.... My major theme is that we hunger for community in the workplace and are a great deal more productive when we find it. To feed this hunger in ways that preserve democratic values of individual dignity, opportunity for all, and mutual support is to harness energy and productivity beyond imagining."

A recent *Harvard Business Review* article entitled "The Knowledge Creating Company" also interests you. In it author Ikujiro Nonaka, a professor of management at Hitotsubashi University in Japan, makes a case for the knowledge-creating organization: "In an economy where the only certainty is uncertainty, the one sure source of lasting competitive advantage is knowledge. When markets shift, technologies proliferate, competitors multiply and products become obsolete almost overnight, successful companies are those that consistently create new knowledge, disseminate it widely throughout the organization, and quickly embody it in new technologies and products. These activities define the 'knowledge-creating' company, whose sole business is continuous innovation. And yet, despite all the talk about 'brainpower' and 'intellectual capital,' few managers grasp the true nature of the knowledge-creating company—let alone know how to manage it. The reason: they misunderstand what knowledge is and what companies must do to exploit it."

International business-school professors Solveig Wikström and Richard Normann, authors of *Knowledge and Value*, also stress the new source of productivity, "The creation of new knowledge and its application in companies does create renewal and growth.... But the supply of knowledge itself is not the only important factor. At least as significant is the ability to absorb, apply and exploit knowledge in new production processes, products and services, new forms of organization and hitherto untried forms of cooperation with customer and suppliers." They go on to point out that "a deeper analysis of what is happening in the world of business today reveals many examples of successful and creative companies which are developing new business logics and new forms of leadership with the help of new technology and unconventional ways of handling knowledge.... Corporate knowledge bearers must learn quickly to create, absorb and apply new knowledge" in organizations where boundaries have become blurred and penetrable.

Finally, *Fortune* magazine's recent cover story, "The End of the Job," makes it abundantly clear that the old way of increasing productivity by eliminating, combining, or even creating jobs won't work in the future. According to the article, few people recognize the extent to which the world of work has changed: "Our organizational world is no longer a pattern of jobs, the way a honeycomb is a pattern of those little hexagonal pockets of honey. In place of jobs, there are part-time and temporary work situations. That change is symptomatic of a deeper change that is subtler but more profound. The deeper change is this: Today's organization is rapidly being transformed from a structure built out of jobs into a field of work needed to be done."

TWO-O'CLOCK-IN-THE-MORNING COURAGE

When you glance up from your reading, the clock on your wall says it's almost 2 A.M. Recalling Napoleon's observation that the real test of a leader's courage comes not in the afternoon of doing battle, but in the dead of night when he or she makes the tough decisions about tomorrow's campaign, you decide it's decision-making time.

Now you revisit the three options you had weighed earlier in the day: focusing your attention over the next several weeks on increasing your own productivity; increasing the productivity of the seven division presidents; or working to increase the productivity of all FaraCom's 1600 employees. To help you decide, you chart the advantages and disadvantages of each option:

Option	Advantages	Disadvantages
1. Personal productivity	Maximizes your own productivity and provides an example for everyone else in the organization	Delays directly helping other executives and employees to increase their own productivity
2. Division presidents' productivity	Builds strong relationships with your executive team and creates the greatest lever for change in the organization	Deals with a group of people with entrenched styles and larger egos, making it difficult to bring about change
3. Companywide productivity	Reaches the greatest number of people the fastest	Requires a large investment of time and resources and may not work without exemplary behavior at the top

As you review the chart summarizing the advantages and disadvantages of each option, you realize that you must eventually accomplish productivity improvements for yourself, for your executive team, and for every person in the FaraCom organization. As the clock keeps ticking however, you also realize you must act decisively by starting somewhere. What do you want to do?

If you decide to focus first and foremost on your own productivity, turn to Chapter 2, page 11.

If you wish to focus on building the productivity of your seven division presidents, turn to Chapter 3, page 15.

If you choose to design a companywide productivity system, turn to Chapter 4, page 21.

CHAPTER 2

Maximizing Your Own Productivity

Once you decide to focus on enhancing your own productivity as the best way to maximize your own strategic leverage and set an example for others in the organization, you use your weekend to read everything you can get your hands on about strategic productivity: Hamel and Prahalad's *The Competitive Future*, Champy's *Reengineering Management*, John Naisbitt's *Global Paradox*, and numerous other books and articles. However, one question sticks with you as you lie in bed at night waiting for sleep: "What's the most valuable thing I can do as CEO of this organization?" As you ponder that question, you recall a book you read years ago by Ken Schatz called *Managing by Influence*. The author used the simple analogy of a lever to illustrate his main point. The longer the handle, the more weight you can move, or, as Archimedes put it, "Give me a long enough lever and a place to stand, and I can move the world." This line of thinking raises yet another question: "What can I do to achieve the greatest impact on the most people inside and outside FaraCom?" Unable to sleep Sunday night, you go into your study and place a blank sheet of paper in the middle of your desk. On it you begin capturing your basic strengths and weaknesses as well as options for improving your strengths and eliminating your weaknesses.

Over the next few weeks, while keeping a close eye on division operations and financial performance, you continue considering your talents and capabilities. You are very project oriented, you like developing new

11

ideas, new thrusts and new directions more than you enjoy implementing, executing, and developing the sort of concrete systems that will crank out tangible results. In other words, you are a highly conceptual person, though you have also demonstrated a knack for orchestrating your ideas and concepts in a way that enables more practical, execution-oriented people to carry them out. Your colleagues over the years have often characterized you as more of a leader than a manager, the sort of person who designs levers others can pull, though Bill Faragut sought your services because he thought he saw in you what he described as "a unique combination of management and leadership skills." As he put it, "I liked the way you led this retreat. You know how to develop managers." You have also gained a reputation for formulating sound strategies and building strong cultures, another plus in Faragut's mind. Still, most of your experience in that regard stems from consulting projects, not from hands-on involvement in a company.

In the past you have been able to step back from a complex business problem and grasp its essence. That ability underscores your basic intuitive nature. You thrive on the challenge of change, although you tend to let external conditions prompt your actions more than you let your own internal vision drive them. Those traits made you an effective consultant, but can you translate those into positive attributes here at FaraCom?

This assessment proves you can look at yourself objectively. You like to think you know yourself and can stay in touch with who you are, with sufficient humility to examine your strengths and your weaknesses dispassionately. Over the years this trait has helped you capitalize on your strengths and minimize the adverse effect of your weaknesses by associating with people who possess complementary capabilities.

With these thoughts in mind, you begin identifying the alternative tracks you might pursue at FaraCom to maximize your own productivity. Eventually, you crystallize your thinking around three basic options: (1) create a strong overall vision and strategic theme for FaraCom that can guide each of the divisions toward prosperous futures; (2) develop strong strategies and cultures in each division; or (3) train each of the seven division presidents to think strategically. Which option will most powerfully leverage your own talents and capabilities? Which will be most consistent with the resources available within FaraCom? Which will provide the greatest value to FaraCom's customers? In short, "Which option will maximize my own productivity?" Your chart of options, based on an analysis of your own strengths and weaknesses, reveals both up sides and down sides for each:

Option	Upsides	Downsides
1. Create a compelling overall vision and strategic theme for FaraCom that can guide each of the divisions to future prosperity.	Provides integrity and continuity across divisions, combining functions and activities where appropriate. Possible strategic themes include offering value-based entertainment to feed the growing demand for nonviolent, nonsexually explicit entertainment.	Could restrict growth and force a competition among divisions that might prove severely limiting.
2. Develop strong strategies and cultures in each division with the help of division presidents.	Allows each division to grow at its own pace and to maximize its own strengths and capabilities, draws upon your own expertise and experience and spreads FaraCom's risk over many businesses.	Could spread you too thin, making it difficult to create a strong senior team. Duplicates time and costs in each division.
3. Train each of the seven division presidents to think strategically.	Gives you the opportunity to become intimately involved with the development and training of each of your seven division presidents, who might greatly benefit from your own experience and ability.	Could prove too indirect an approach to get the kind of results that Bill Faragut demands in the short term.

As you stare at this chart, you keep coming back to the basic issue of leverage. Which of the three options will most effectively deploy your talents and capabilities and, thereby, maximize your contribution as CEO of FaraCom? Your ultimate choice must take into account the needs of your division presidents, the long-range goals of the whole corporation, and the satisfaction of FaraCom's customers. Of course, it must also account for your own personal needs and goals, which include both your success as a leader and the financial rewards that success will garner. Content that you have laid the groundwork for a wise decision, you look forward to a relaxing weekend. When you awake Monday morning, however, you find that the decision has not made itself, as you had hoped it would. Now, you simply must pick a course of action. What will you do?

If you decide to pursue an integrated strategy and theme for all FaraCom divisions, turn to Chapter 5, page 25.

If you want to develop strategic plans and strong cultures in each of the divisions, turn to Chapter 6, page 29.

If you would rather train your seven division presidents to think strategically, turn to Chapter 7, page 33.

CHAPTER 3

Increasing the Productivity of Division Presidents

Having chosen to focus on increasing the productivity of your seven division presidents, you begin weighing different ideas and methods for tackling such a tricky undertaking. A number of options occur to you: You could invite the division presidents to develop their own productivity-improvement agendas and schedules, you could assess each division president in terms of psychological type, to determine what kind of productivity increases and enhancements might work best for each individual, or you could employ an outside consultant to design a program for the group. Given the fact that you will be trying to change the way mature executives with highly developed egos work, you know you will run into a certain amount of resistance, if not downright hostility. As you get better acquainted with your division presidents, your concern mounts.

For two weeks you have spent enough unstructured, unplanned time with each of the seven division presidents to get a feel for their distinct personalities, which you summarize using David Keirsey and Marilyn Bates's classification of psychological temperaments, published in their book *Please Understand Me: Character and Temperament Types.* The Keirsey and Bates classification system includes four basic types:

SP = Sensing and Perceiving
SJ = Sensing and Judging
NT = Intuitive and Thinking
NF = Intuitive and Feeling

Sean Cope, president of cable television operations, exhibits the temperament of an SP (sensing and perceiving). Basically, he's impulsive. According to Keirsey and Bates, SPs behave impulsively because doing so makes them feel alive. They love their impulses and the exhilaration they feel as their impulses well up inside them. While SPs pursue goals and form relationships with others, they can easily abandon them and take off in other directions if expectations and ties become too binding. Like SPs, Cope loves freedom and independence, and, since he easily becomes bored with the *status quo*, he frequently varies his work patterns, seeks out random experiences, tries new foods, and takes unusual vacations. He hungers for action without the constraints of rules or practice, thriving on circumstances with unknown outcomes or results. Because he lives by his impulses and acts spontaneously on those impulses, living for the moment, he tends to repudiate long-term goals, objectives, and plans. To his credit these traits have served Sean Cope well in the rapidly changing environment of cable television, where he can justify a different project every week, a new location every month, and a kaleidoscope of focuses. However, you wonder whether Sean can modify his approach when the time comes for building the structure and systems that must inevitably become a more important part of his division's future.

Mona Sork, president of retail operations, and Alan Peay, president of magazine publishing, both exhibit the SJ (sensing and judging) temperament, which, according to Keirsey and Bates, manifests itself in a longing for usefully serving the social unit to which they belong. Like all SJs, Sork and Peay want to belong, but they also want their belonging to be earned. They never want to feel derelict or negligent in their duty. They are givers, not receivers, taking care of people and situations, and they constantly seek out binding obligations to do so. Hierarchical structures appeal to them, and nothing pleases them more than establishing and maintaining institutions that foster the continuity of social units—family, church, service clubs, corporations, governments. At FaraCom, Sork and Peay have won reputations as great conservators who have used their authority to conserve and perpetuate heritage, tradition, and standards. More than Bill Faragut himself, these two have become the caretakers of the FaraCom culture. Both exhibit clear SJ temperaments with which they have established two of the most profitable divisions at FaraCom. However, you wonder whether they can adapt their cautious temperaments to the massive changes taking place in both the retail and magazine-publishing industries.

David Zollweg, president of software and CD-ROM publishing, and Janice Kofoed, president of catalog sales and direct marketing, exhibit the

NT (intuitive and thinking) temperament. According to Keirsey and Bates, power fascinates this type of person—not power over people, but power over circumstances and nature. Like all NTs, Zollweg and Kofoed long to understand, predict, explain, and control reality. Since they worship competence, they constantly seek intelligence and wisdom in their respective domains. Quite often they report feeling on the verge of failure, and they suffer a pervasive sense of inadequacy. Ever searching for the why's of the universe, they strive so hard to perform competently that they usually succeed in their endeavors, particularly in the areas of science, technology, design and engineering, R&D, management, and philosophy. Both Zollweg and Kofoed exhibit this obsession running their divisions. Zollweg charts new waters and introduces exciting new software and CD-ROM products at a feverish pace, while Kofoed continues to build a state-of-the-art direct marketing and sales machine that will benefit FaraCom for years to come. You suspect, however, that these two high-powered thinkers will soon want to move on to greater challenges. Can you keep them challenged and contributing, here at FaraCom?

Stephen Ferreira, president of film and video production, and Lisa Harshaw, president of book publishing, exhibit the NF (intuitive and feeling) temperament, which prompts them to pursue the hard-to-explain goal of becoming. According to Keirsey and Bates, NFs hunger for self-actualization and self-realization. In other words, they continually search for their "real" selves or the "true" goal. Their perpetual searches often take circular routes as they constantly seek to satisfy their deep desires for unity with a perfect whole and a uniqueness of identity in that whole. Ferreira's and Harshaw's powerful influence on the minds of others in the organization stems from the essence of their work, which involves literature, art, music, film, and other artistic products. They desire to inspire and persuade by examining the meaning of life, identifying what's significant to mankind, and searching for self. Their creative talents win ardent followers for their programs. Over the years, both have made great personal sacrifices, sometimes ruthlessly, in order to help others find their way. Demanding direct or indirect communication with others, they strive tirelessly toward a vision of perfection. Ferreira and Harshaw inspire their divisions with their visions. Ferreira strives to produce films and videos that lift the human spirit, while Harshaw wants to publish only books that impart meaning and value to readers, helping them in one way or another. Ferreira and Harshaw have become close friends and often wonder why the other division presidents don't share their passion or vision. As these two divisions grow, you wonder whether Ferreira or Harshaw can provide the necessary structure, systems, and goals to keep other personality types motivated and directed. Right now these divisions run on passion. How long can that last?

As you think about these seven division presidents and their respective temperaments, you realize that any productivity program must account for their temperaments, but how much so? Can the SPs and NFs become more like the SJs? Can the NTs develop NF characteristics? Can you increase the productivity of each of these executives without losing the very traits that have made them successful in the past?

To help visualize your thinking, you construct a chart that lists three options for action, along with the pros and cons of each.

Option	*Pros*	*Cons*
1. Should you let division presidents set their own productivity agendas?	• Freedom • Customization • Relevance • Creativity • Nonthreatening • Mature Approach	• Loose • Unstructured • No Guidelines or Standards • Hard to Manage
2. Should you further assess the psychological type of each division president to determine the productivity program?	• Research Based • Sophisticated Tools • Scientific and Rational • Meaningful • Long-lasting	• Takes Time • Requires Commitment • Dependence Upon Evaluation Instruments • Potential for Misuse
3. Should you hire an outside consultant to design a productivity program for the group?	• Clear Objectives • Expert-Based • Common Framework • Latest Thinking	• Expensive • Requires Buy-In • Demands Constant Follow-up • Consultants are a Crutch

As you consider your summary of pros and cons, you grapple with the basic issues related to productivity. How do you really improve productivity in someone else? How do you recognize productivity levels? How can you best measure productivity? Though you feel that the three options you've identified could get results for you and FaraCom, you can't decide which one to choose, so you talk with each of your seven division presidents, probing each gently, without specifically raising the three options, to determine which might work best.

As you think about your experience with the seven division presidents, carefully reviewing their personality profiles, you realize that Sean Cope, David Zollweg, and Janice Kofoed would probably favor option one (letting division presidents set their own productivity agendas), while Stephen Ferreira and Lisa Harshaw would most likely favor option two (using further assessments of psychological type to determine productivity programs), and Mona Sork and Alan Peay would gladly welcome the assistance of an outside consultant. This makes your decision tougher because now you know that no matter which option you choose, some executives will resist it. Once again, only you can decide.

If you choose to allow each of the seven division presidents to set individual agendas for productivity improvement, turn to Chapter 8, page 37.

If you prefer to further assess the psychological type of each division president and use that evaluation to determine productivity-improvement programs for each, turn to Chapter 9, page 41.

If you decide to hire an outside consultant to design a productivity program for the group, turn to Chapter 10, page 49.

CHAPTER 4

Building Productivity Throughout the Entire Organization

Convinced that you must achieve higher levels of productivity throughout FaraCom, you immediately begin searching for the right productivity-enhancement tools you can apply to every level of the organization. After several weeks of reviewing a number of available tools and programs by visiting numerous companies and hiring two consultants to survey everything on the market, you boil the possibilities down to three: Franklin Quest's time management program, Covey Leadership's priority management system, or EmpowerTech's personal productivity technology.

The Franklin Quest system offers the highly successful Franklin Day Planner, used by individuals and corporations for more than a decade, as well as the company's newly developed productivity-improvement systems built around the day-planning system. The strengths of the Franklin approach include its strong reputation, ease of use, training and support, and the option of paper-based or electronic systems. Its major weakness lies in its narrow time management emphasis. And, while you know that Franklin consultants can help your organization use their tools, productivity improvements will still depend upon the people within FaraCom.

The Covey Leadership system focuses more on priorities and principles, helping people to identify why they do what they do. The strength of this system stems from its principle-based approach and the guidance it gives people to focus on priorities, as described in Stephen Covey's new book, *First Things First*. The major weakness of Covey system lies in the extent of its limited support and training. The Covey organization primarily employs *The Seven Habits of Highly Effective People* program and provides consulting on organizational and managerial effectiveness. While the company assures you that they are building the staff to support their daily priority management system, it has not yet proven itself as thoroughly as Franklin's. Success of the Covey system would of course depend on the people within FaraCom embracing its basic concepts.

The EmpowerTech system harnesses a new technology in the form of a notebook-sized phone-fax-computer with specialized software for E-mail, productivity tracking, project scheduling, priority assessment, results output and psychological testing. EmpowerTech puts a wide array of the most up-to-date tools for improving productivity in the hands of every employee in an organization, making productivity a commonly held, daily experience. The strengths of the EmpowerTech system lie in the technology and software that make productivity a common cause within the organization, allowing everyone to assess their own productivity and monitor it against others. The EmpowerTech system also includes a software program called "Whole Picture" that relates an individual worker's activities to the overall progress, results, strategy, and culture of the organization. The major weakness of the EmpowerTech system lies in getting people to use the technology and make it a daily habit. This system would take the longest to implement and cost the most. You prepare this summary of the strengths and weaknesses of each of the three alternatives:

Option	*Strength*	*Weakness*
1. Franklin Quest System	Proven usefulness and extensive training support	Overemphasis on time
2. Covey Leadership System	First things first emphasis and principle-centered approach	Insufficient training support
3. EmpowerTech System	Total integration of productivity improvement systems through technology	Cost and length of time for implementation

As you ponder the three possibilities at length, you wish you could spend more time with the seven division presidents discussing the pros and cons, but your relationship with them has not sufficiently developed to allow for meaningful, open communication. However, you have developed some initial impressions: Mona Sork and Alan Peay seem highly organized and decisive; David Zollweg and Janice Kofoed are intellectually oriented, with strong desires for independence; Sean Cope worships freedom but adapts well to changing circumstances; and Lisa Harshaw and Stephen Ferreira both see themselves as corporate artists, working hard to apply their crafts of book publishing and film making.

In addition, you want each of them to keep running his or her own division, and you hesitate drawing them into corporatewide decisions before you know where you yourself want to go. Developing a team environment at the top will take a lot longer than you expected and may prove impossible, given the diversity and autonomy of FaraCom's businesses. You may actually prefer maintaining a high degree of decentralization among each of the divisions, which in and of itself would influence your selection of a companywide productivity improvement system. The Franklin Quest system would probably work best in a highly decentralized organization because of its easy implementation and access to training support. The EmpowerTech system would probably require more coordination across the entire company to make the system most effective. Still, the EmpowerTech system could work on a division basis as well. The Covey Leadership system could function in either a decentralized or an integrated structure. After some additional consideration, you decide that decentralization should drive FaraCom's organizational structure. You also conclude, however, that one common value should permeate all FaraCom operations: productivity improvement and maximization. Now you must decide which of the three options will best accomplish your goals.

If you wish to implement Franklin Quest's time-management program, turn to Chapter 11, page 53.

If you choose to use Covey Leadership's priority-management system, turn to Chapter 12, page 57.

If you decide to employ EmpowerTech's technology and software, turn to Chapter 13, page 61.

CHAPTER 5

Creating an Integrated Strategy and Theme

Convinced that developing an integrated strategic direction and theme will both benefit all the FaraCom divisions and best deploy your own capabilities, you begin laying the groundwork with each of your seven division presidents by persuasively articulating the need for integration among their units. While Alan Peay, president of magazine publishing, and Mona Sork, president of retail operations, along with Sean Cope, president of cable television operations, agree that a coordinated theme makes sense, the other division presidents, David Zollweg, president of software and CD-ROM publishing, Janice Kofoed, president of catalog sales and direct marketing, Stephen Ferreira, president of film and video production, and Lisa Harshaw, president of book publishing, see it as an encroachment upon their turf. You attempt to address their concerns by discussing the matter with them one on one, arguing that the productivity of the entire organization depends upon everyone pulling in the same direction and thereby gaining the maximum strategic leverage in the marketplace. "Customer sharing" (i.e., the offering of numerous products and services to the same customer base) will, you argue, provide the key to FaraCom's future, and the company can attain this kind of "strategic productivity" only when everyone in the organization steadfastly pursues a similar strategic vision, making it possible for diverse and even disparate operations to accomplish more than they could on their own.

As the four opposing division presidents begin to soften up to your point of view, you decide to hold a retreat with all seven division presidents to explore possible unifying themes for the company. Out of the retreat emerges a semblance of consensus around the concept of producing and distributing books, magazines, films, videos, software, and CD-ROMs directed at the growing "values-based" market segment. The values-based market segment includes customers who have become more and more disenchanted with the violence and erotica of Hollywood and are searching for more wholesome, uplifting entertainment. Well-known film critics such as Michael Medved have helped identify this emerging market, and you yourself believe that not only Americans, but consumers throughout the world, will respond to products that promote traditional values, spiritual and mental well being, and quality of life. "Tapping into this trend could make a lot of sense for us," you tell your division presidents at the end of the meeting.

When asked for examples of how this would work within the company, you respond that in the area of publishing books, Lisa Harshaw could pursue titles similar to *Soul Mates, The Road Less Traveled, First Things First, Everything I Know I Learned in Kindergarten,* and so forth. In the film and video area, Stephen Ferreira could concentrate on making films similar to *Shadowlands, Remains of the Day, Dead Poets' Society, Chariots of Fire, It Could Happen to You,* and other PG- or G-rated movies. In the software and CD-ROM markets, David Zollweg could focus on products such as *Encarta, Dangerous Creatures, Art Gallery,* and other "edutainment" titles. In the magazine publishing area, Alan Peay could consciously direct new and existing publications toward family values, family life, spirituality, perhaps even designing magazines geared toward more conservative audiences. In the cable television arena, the VISN Network and others have developed programming that taps into this market, and Sean Cope could do the same. Janice Kofoed could position catalog sales and direct marketing in this same market by identifying values-based lists and market segments to which her division can provide a wide variety of appealing products, and Mona Sork could focus retail operations, over time, on promoting values-based products across all categories, including books, tapes, software, videos—a move similar to that of Media Play or Hastings, but geared specifically to the values-based market.

While your seven division presidents slowly but surely warm up to the idea of a common strategic theme, they argue that it will take time to effect the necessary shifts, given the disparate directions of so many current operations. Sensing their growing support, however, you ask them to think carefully about the potential benefits of a coordinated and integrated strategy. "Imagine," you say, "the impact of such a theme on our overall productivity."

"I can see it," responds Alan Peay, president of magazine publishing. "We now spend far too much time in this organization making our separate cases for investment in new projects, competing with one another for dollars that push us in totally different directions. Tightening the scope of products could double our productivity overnight." Janice Kofoed, president of catalog sales and direct marketing, agrees, saying, "We could develop a direct marketing machine geared to the values-based market that could outcompete every other form of distribution in the communications and entertainment industry." Sean Cope adds, "Speaking for cable television operations, the opportunities for tapping into this demand for wholesome, quality entertainment offers tremendous potential. I happen to know that *Readers Digest* is looking for a partner to establish a cable network that could exploit this new strategy perfectly." When others respond similarly, you feel you are making strong progress toward capturing the kind of strategic productivity you have envisioned.

In the months that follow, you and your seven division presidents work out a comprehensive strategic vision and plan for FaraCom that will focus all of its business activities on serving the needs of the values-based market. Much of the strategic planning process deals with transitioning from current conflicting positions to a more coordinated strategic focus, which you anticipate will take the rest of the current year. Not until the second year do you think FaraCom will see any real effects of the integrated strategy. At the end of your first year as CEO, sales increase to $560 million, with a slight improvement in profits, as shown in the following table:

Selected Financial and Productivity Information
(Revenues and Profits in $ Millions)

	First Year	*Previous Year*
Revenues	$560	$508
Profits	($18)	($22)
Employees	1,653	1,612
Revenues per Employee (Actual $)	$338,778	$315,136
Profits per Employee (Actual $)	($10,889)	($13,648)

The numbers, coupled with your division presidents' confidence in the new direction, impress Bill Faragut and the other members of the board sufficiently that they agree to support your continued search for strategic productivity.

During your second year as CEO, you work closely with each of the seven division presidents to develop strategies for each division that link together under the theme of serving the values-based market. To your delight, they purchase new values-oriented customer lists, initiate a number of exciting research projects, pursue purchasing the rights to specific new films, and begin a new thrust in magazine development and book publishing. During the ebb and flow of the intensified planning and preparation for striking out in the new direction, you continue to reassure the seven division presidents, who in turn reassure their people, that the advantage of such strategic integration will allow people to double, even triple, their productivity through the sheer simplicity and clarity of FaraCom's strategic mission.

After months of intense effort, you feel that FaraCom can fully launch its new integrated strategy. Much of the groundwork has already begun to bear fruit as the company readies new books, films, videos, software, CD-ROMs, and magazines for the market, all driven by the new philosophy. A new direct-marketing program aimed directly at the values-based market looks especially promising. At year's end, sales increase to $620 million, with profits up modestly to $2 million, as shown below:

Selected Financial and Productivity Information
(Revenues and Profits in $ Millions)

	Second Year	First Year
Revenues	$620	$560
Profits	$2	($18)
Employees	1,718	1,653
Revenues per Employee (Actual $)	$360,885	$338,778
Profits per Employee (Actual $)	$1,164	($10,889)

A few important members of the board grow anxious over these numbers and demand further assurance from you that the next year will finally achieve the tremendous payoff you have been promising. You attempt to do so during a three-hour discussion at the year-end board meeting, but after your presentation you still sense some uneasiness among the more skeptical board members. Later that evening, Bill Faragut calls you at home to say he's decided that the board needs a full assessment of the company's productivity and that he has already hired an outside firm to conduct that assessment. While this development surprises you, you feel so confident that the results will support your decisions over the past two years that you agree to the undertaking without batting an eye. The next morning you inform your seven division presidents about the impending assessment and ask for their full cooperation during the next 30-day period.

Go to Chapter 14, page 65, to discover the results of the companywide assessment of current productivity.

CHAPTER 6

Developing Strong Divisional Strategies and Cultures

Given your own strong experience in strategic thinking and corporate culture building, albeit as an outside consultant, you decide to apply this strength to each division of the organization, helping your division presidents forge strong strategies and cultures for their units. When you announce your decision to each of your seven division presidents, you make it clear that you will not usurp their responsibility and authority for developing their units' strategies and cultures. While some express skepticism, particularly Sean Cope, president of cable television operations, Mona Sork, president of retail operations, Alan Peay, president of magazine publishing, and Janice Kofoed, president of catalog sales and direct marketing, you feel that your coaching will quickly dissipate those feelings as Cope, Sork, Peay, and Kofoed begin to realize the benefits of this approach to productivity.

You lay out a master schedule, beginning with Janice Kofoed, president of catalog sales and direct marketing, that allows you to spend in-depth time with each of the seven division presidents and their management teams over the next six months. Coaching one division at a time, you act more like an outside consultant than a CEO as you oversee strategic analyses and culture audits and help generate alternatives, establish criteria for decision making, build support among the management team, and lay the

29

groundwork for implementation. After all, you tell yourself, a CEO in today's decentralized, autonomous, empowered, networked organization must work more like a management consultant or facilitator, coaching rather than commanding and controlling the way CEOs did ten years ago. Janice Kofoed responds enthusiastically to your experienced guidance and communicates to the other seven division presidents that your nonthreatening style and approach has begun to pay off for her division. You started with her division because you knew that Kofoed's endorsement would influence the others, but the extent of her enthusiasm does surprise you.

It takes you almost 12 months to get all seven divisions moving in the new direction, but by the end of your first year as CEO, you see promising results. At year end, sales increase to $600 million and profits pass break-even, as shown below:

Selected Financial and Productivity Information
(Revenues and Profits in $ Millions)

	First Year	Previous Year
Revenues	$600	$508
Profits	$.5	($22)
Employees	1,664	1,612
Revenues per Employee (Actual $)	$360,577	$315,136
Profits per Employee (Actual $)	$300	($13,648)

With a solid basis for strong strategies and cultures established in each of the seven divisions, you turn your attention during the second year of your tenure at FaraCom to implementation, helping each division president develop monitoring and measurement systems to provide early warning flags on execution problems. As you shift your emphasis from planning to action, you reinforce the basic idea that execution determines 70 percent of the success of this sort of undertaking. In an off-site meeting with your division presidents, you observe, "For the last year we've focused on improving strategic productivity; this year we must shift our focus to operational productivity."

One by one, the seven divisions earnestly begin implementing their revitalized and crystallized strategies and cultures. The catalog sales and direct-marketing division, under Janice Kofoed's direction, assumes a strong supporting posture with the other divisions, marketing their products with a new vigor and a deeper sense of service. Stephen Ferreira's film- and video production division positions itself to produce films at a cost of $1 to $2 million targeted at the cable television and video-rental markets, which the catalog sales and direct marketing division can easily reach via FaraCom's growing database of customers. Lisa Harshaw, president of book publishing, pursues a course that ties film and video production to book publishing, but she also launches a new project called "The World's One Hundred Best Books," offering them simultaneously in video and audio formats and in book form with original reproductions of first printings. David Zollweg, president of software and CD-ROM publishing, builds on his division's past focus on combining education and entertainment in what he calls "edutainment products" that combine learning and fun in revolutionary new ways, such as the "Field Trip" series, which takes children, ages 3 to 10, on exciting adventures into the worlds of firefighting, road construction, ballet, and horse ranching. The magazine publishing division, under the direction of Alan Peay, builds on its track record of specialty magazines in a variety of areas by working with Janice Kofoed to understand the needs and desires of FaraCom's growing database, identifying new opportunities to serve the needs of those customers. One product, a new *Great Literature* magazine, ties directly into "The World's One Hundred Best Books" program being developed by Lisa Harshaw and Stephen Ferreira. Mona Sork, president of retail operations, pursues a radically new strategy, consolidating retail operations, closing stores, and moving to a cable-based shoppers' network, working with Janice Kofoed and Sean Cope to take advantage of the increasing number of shoppers ordering from their homes. Sean Cope, president of cable television operations, launches a new "Classics Network" in conjunction with other divisions and also begins entering into numerous alliances with magazines throughout the world to create a "Magazine Network" that should eventually spawn numerous subnetworks over the next several years.

By the end of your second year as CEO, sales climb to $700 million, with profits increasing to $10 million, as shown by the following graph:

Selected Financial and Productivity Information
(Revenues and Profits in $ Millions)

	Second Year	*First Year*
Revenues	$702	$600
Profits	$10	$.5
Employees	1,875	1,664
Revenues per Employee (Actual $)	$374,400	$360,577
Profits per Employee (Actual $)	$5,333	$300

Bill Faragut and the board seem pleased with your performance, but after they review the year-end results, Bill asks you to undertake a major assessment of productivity throughout the organization in order to, as he puts it, "provide a solid benchmark for the future." You agree to the organization-wide productivity assessment, believing it will prove the wisdom of your decisions over the past two years. While you believe that your example of productivity improvement through effective self-deployment has encouraged each of your division presidents to emphasize what they can do best in their own divisions to move them forward, you wonder whether you've focused specifically and directly enough on increasing productivity. Have your efforts to increase your own personal productivity sufficiently influenced the rest of the organization?

To learn the results of the organizationwide productivity assessment, turn to Chapter 14, page 65.

CHAPTER 7

Training Your Seven Division Presidents to Think Strategically

---

Given your own major strength—your strategic thinking ability—you decide that training your seven division presidents to do so represents the most valuable self-deployment and personal productivity track you can pursue in your tenure as FaraCom's CEO. To initiate strategic training and development, you institute two vital elements: first, a revised business-planning process and, second, a rigorous schedule of strategy sessions, plan reviews, staff meetings, and one-on-one interviews aimed at strengthening the strategic thinking and positioning capabilities of your seven division presidents. The new business-planning process focuses on economic and strategic logic, requiring your seven division presidents to think constantly of the fundamental strategic and economic variables active in each of their businesses. You expect the business-planning process to bring more rigorous disciplined thinking, as well as more creativity to bear on divisional decision making. You launch the new business-planning process with a set of guidelines that asks thought-provoking questions designed to guide the thinking of division presidents and their management teams as they develop annual business plans. You also conduct intense strategy sessions with each of the divisions that formally kick off the business-planning process and help divisional management teams stretch their strategic-thinking capabilities earlier in the process.

In each initial strategy session, you and FaraCom's senior managers play *The Strategy Game*, an "interactive business simulation designed to test and improve strategic decision making." This simulation will, you hope, loosen up the group and prepare them for the real thing. The experience turns out even better than you hoped as the top 50 executives and managers at FaraCom begin to improve decision making by expanding their "bandwidth" and their "focusdepth" (the extent to which they weigh alternatives and implications when making a decision). While the game requires decision making in a binary mode (i.e., a player picks one of only two choices at any given decision point), you make it clear to everyone that in a real-life situation, a fuller range of choices will crop up day in and day out. You encourage these 50 executives and managers to expand and strengthen their decision making so that they can avoid making inappropriate, premature, incomplete, or half-baked decisions, thereby substantially improving productivity in the long run.

As you watch the level of strategic thinking rise within FaraCom, you're pleased that your training and development efforts seem to be taking hold among your seven division presidents and their teams. However, you also begin to see a deterioration in operational efficiencies and effectiveness as some divisions become overly preoccupied with strategic-thinking and planning at the expense of operational considerations. Though you had anticipated this possibility when you launched your strategic-thinking program, you don't recognize the full extent of the problem until the end of your first year as CEO, when revenues barely increase to $540 million with only a modest improvement in profits, as shown below:

Selected Financial and Productivity Information
(Revenues and Profits in $ Millions)

	First Year	*Previous Year*
Revenues	$540	$508
Profits	($20)	($22)
Employees	1,686	1,612
Revenues per Employee (Actual $)	$320,285	$315,136
Profits per Employee (Actual $)	($11,862)	($13,648)

Given these disappointing results, you determine during your second year to try shifting your emphasis to operational issues, hoping that your earlier attention to strategic issues has taken hold and will remain strong. Unfortunately, your seven division presidents see the shift as pressure from

Bill Faragut and the board for more short-term gains, and they begin questioning your emphasis on strategic thinking. Perhaps, they tell you, we wasted too much time last year on work that won't really bear fruit. You fight this perception for several months while at the same time attempting to shore up operational effectiveness and results, but you make little headway convincing your division presidents that strategic thinking makes the primary difference.

By the end of your second year as CEO, you know that you face, at best, a set of mixed reviews on your performance as CEO. Sales reach $598 million and profits approach break-even, as shown below:

Selected Financial and Productivity Information
(Revenues and Profits in $ Millions)

	First Year	Previous Year
Revenues	$598	$540
Profits	($5)	($20)
Employees	1,842	1,686
Revenues per Employee (Actual $)	$324,647	$320,285
Profits per Employee (Actual $)	($2,714)	($11,862)

In light of this performance, Bill Faragut insists on a complete evaluation of where FaraCom stands as an organization, with a particular emphasis on productivity. You agree to the companywide assessment, but wonder how it will reflect upon your leadership.

To get a preliminary reading from your seven division presidents, you conduct an interview with each to find out where they stand. Sean Cope, president of cable television operations, says, "Getting sidetracked away from a focus on operations has simply convinced me that too much strategic thinking creates more problems than it solves." Mona Sork, president of retail operations, suggests, "You need to provide more structure for the planning, integrating it with operations so that strategic thinking and positioning don't stand alone, but inform FaraCom's overall structure and business processes." Alan Peay, president of magazine publishing, echoes Mona's concerns when he adds that "the business-planning process you instituted works, but it needs to be modified to include operational, financial, and human-resource planning as well. We simply can't take our eyes off operations." David Zollweg, president of software and CD-ROM publishing, disagrees, saying, "I think you shifted away from your emphasis on strategic thinking too soon. You buckled under to pressure from Bill Faragut when operations didn't deliver short-term improvements. You should stick to your guns—your program was working." Janice Kofoed, president of catalog sales and direct marketing, sides with Zollweg, offering, "I think the system of business planning and strategy sessions was brilliant. It changed my whole way of thinking about the economic logic of direct sales and allowed me to get a firmer hold on how we create value for customers. Don't get bogged down in operational minutia. That's what got us in hot water in the first place." Stephen Ferreira, president of film and video production, offers yet another view when he says, "The only concern I have right now stems from the reality that people feel confused. They're wondering about FaraCom's real focus. They're getting mixed signals about strategic thinking and operational effectiveness, and that's paralyzing them." Finally, Lisa Harshaw, president of book publishing, summarizes her view of the situation: "You've made a definite impact on our strategic thinking, but now we should blend strategic and operational concerns to improve the bottom line and give everyone a sense of constancy."

With this input from your seven division presidents, you look forward to the productivity assessment and developing your next wave of productivity enhancements at FaraCom. Most of your division presidents believe productivity has increased at FaraCom because of your focus on strategic thinking; they just need more time to translate it to the bottom line.

To discover the results of the companywide productivity assessment, turn to Chapter 14, page 65.

CHAPTER 8

Allowing the Seven Division Presidents to Set Their Own Agendas

After reading Hammer and Champy's new book, *Reengineering Management,* you convince yourself that giving your seven division presidents maximum autonomy to set their own agendas for increased productivity will accomplish better results than anything else. When you tell each of them that you intend to give them a free hand in setting their productivity improvement agendas, they respond with mixed reactions. Sean Cope, president of cable television operations, loves the idea because he never likes to be controlled or told what to do. Mona Sork, president of retail operations, on the other hand, lives and dies by the organizational hierarchy imposed from above, and she believes that giving too much freedom to the seven presidents will cause too much turmoil and prevent the productivity increases you desire. Alan Peay, president of magazine publishing, also feels that more structure will increase productivity at FaraCom. He runs a tight ship and expects everybody else to do the same. David Zollweg, president of software and CD-ROM publishing, favors the idea wholeheartedly and promises that he will do everything in his power to build productivity in his division. Janice Kofoed, your president of catalog sales and direct marketing, assures you that she will have set her agenda for increasing productivity within a week. Stephen Ferreira, president of film and video production, reminds you that not every one of your division presidents will respond in the same way to this opportunity to set their own agendas. He suggests that you may want to monitor some of the division presidents more

37

than others as they set about the task. Finally, Lisa Harshaw, president of book publishing, accepts this approach and tells you that she will focus on people and relationship development to ensure a more cohesive, united front in her division, thus allowing for increased productivity across the board.

Over the next several months, you monitor the agendas set by your seven division presidents to see how well they're improving productivity in their operations. However, when the end-of-the-year figures reveal only lackluster results, Stephen Ferreira and David Zollweg remind you, once again, that not everybody responds well to a free reign. Sales reach $536 million and profits remain the same by year-end, as shown below:

Selected Financial and Productivity Information
(Revenues and Profits in $ Millions)

	First Year	Previous Year
Revenues	$536	$508
Profits	($21)	($22)
Employees	1,642	1,612
Revenues per Employee (Actual $)	$326,431	$315,136
Profits per Employee (Actual $)	($12,789)	($13,648)

At the beginning of your second year as CEO, you spend time with each of your seven presidents, trying to assess their productivity improvement efforts. You discover that Mona Sork and Alan Peay, presidents of retail operations and magazine publishing, respectively, need much more of a framework—more guidance and more structure—to implement their agendas. Neither one of them has done much to improve productivity. Sean Cope, president of cable television operations, has also continued his operation pretty much as usual in his accustomed "constant-crises" mode and has not achieved much improvement in productivity. David Zollweg and Janice Kofoed, heads of software and CD-ROM publishing and catalog sales and direct marketing, have created highly logical systems for improving productivity, but both executives lack the people-development skills that might make their new systems work. Finally, Stephen Ferreira and Lisa

Harshaw, who preside over film and video production and book publishing, prove most effective in developing productivity-improvement paths for their respective divisions because they have both emphasized people development and people interaction and have created an environment where people feel they are doing meaningful work.

During a three-day retreat on Hilton Head Island, you ask Stephen Ferreira and Lisa Harshaw to share their experiences with the other five division presidents, and their presentations launch the group into an intense discussion of alternative agendas for improving productivity. The sharing of ideas and approaches proves quite beneficial as all the division presidents gain new awareness of their different styles and approaches. At the end of the retreat, you invite your seven presidents once again to set their own agendas for improving productivity, making it clear that improved results must occur by the end of the year. You are thankful that by the end of your second year as CEO, sales pass $600 million, with profits improving, as shown below:

Selected Financial and Productivity Information
(Revenues and Profits in $ Millions)

	Second Year	*First Year*
Revenues	$602	$536
Profits	($2)	($21)
Employees	1,709	1,642
Revenues per Employee (Actual $)	$352,253	$326,431
Profits per Employee (Actual $)	($1,170)	($12,789)

Not surprisingly, however, Bill Faragut cites these figures as proof that you need to obtain a companywide assessment of productivity gains to find out exactly where the company stands and how it has positioned itself for the future. While you find this intrusive and think Faragut is overstepping his bounds as chairman of the board, you comply with his suggestion, hoping that your recent efforts to improve the productivity enhancement agendas in each of the divisions will prove satisfactory.

To find out about the results of the companywide productivity assessment, turn to Chapter 14, page 65.

CHAPTER 9

Identifying the Psychological Type of Each Division President

Certain that the personalities of individuals determine the way in which they improve their productivity, you decide to undertake a thorough assessment of the psychological type of each division president. You believe that if you can convince your seven presidents that their type and temperament strongly influence their performance and productivity, then they will carry that message throughout the organization. To start the ball rolling, you hire a group of human resource specialists certified in psychological testing to administer the complete Myers-Briggs Type Indicator (MBTI) to your division presidents. With luck, the process will provide greater clarity and validation of your earlier preassessment using Keirsey and Bates's four temperaments.

As you prepare your seven division presidents for the test, all appear willing to participate, although Sean Cope and Alan Peay seem somewhat skeptical. Stephen Ferreira and Lisa Harshaw, on the other hand, relish the prospect of using an assessment instrument like the MBTI to form the basis of productivity improvement throughout the company. The other division presidents appear somewhat neutral about it. To ease any misgivings, you make it clear that you are committed to helping each of them increase their personal productivity as the first step toward increasing the productivity of others in the organization. None of the seven division presidents disagrees with that goal because they realize that today, more than ever, the example of the leader shapes the development of the culture.

With the help of the outside specialists, each of your seven presidents completes a written assessment and undergoes two or three interviews, all of which result in a fully validated assessment for each of them. You discover that Sean Cope, president of cable television operations, tests out as an "ESFP" (Extraverted Sensing with Feeling), described in the Myers-Briggs "Introduction to Type" as follows:

> ESFP people are friendly, adaptable realists. They rely on what they can see, hear, and know firsthand. They good-naturedly accept and use the facts around them, whatever these are. They look for a satisfying solution instead of trying to impose any "should" or "must" of their own. They are sure that a solution will turn up once they have grasped all of the facts.

> ESFPs do best in careers needing realism, action, and adaptability. Examples are health services, sales, design, transportation, entertainment, secretarial or office work, food services, supervising work groups, machine operation, and many kinds of troubleshooting.

Mona Sork, president of retail operations, shows up as an "ESTJ" (Extraverted Thinking with Sensing):

> ESTJ people use their thinking to run as much of the world as may be theirs to run. They like to organize projects and then act to get things done. Reliance on thinking makes them logical, analytical, objectively critical, and not likely to be convinced by anything but reasoning. They tend to focus on the job, not the people behind the job.

> ESTJs like jobs where the results of their work are immediate, visible, and tangible. They have a natural bent for business, industry, production, and construction. They enjoy administration, where they can set goals, make decisions, and give the necessary orders. Getting things done is their strong suit.

Alan Peay, president of magazine publishing, proves to be an "ISTJ" (Introverted Sensing with Thinking):

> People with ISTJ preferences are extremely dependable and have a complete, realistic, and practical respect for the facts. They absorb, remember, and use any number of facts and are careful about their accuracy. When they see that something needs to be done, they accept the responsibility, often beyond the call of duty. They like everything

clearly stated. Their private reactions, which seldom show in their faces, are often vivid and intense.

ISTJs often choose careers where their talents for organization and accuracy are rewarded. Examples are accounting, civil engineering, law, production, construction, health careers, and office work. They often move into supervisory and management roles.

David Zollweg, president of software and CD-ROM publishing, turns out to exemplify an "INTJ" (Introverted Intuition with Thinking):

People with INTJ preferences are relentless innovators in thought as well as action. They trust their intuitive insights into the true relationships and meanings of things, regardless of established authority or popularly accepted beliefs. Their faith in their inner vision can move mountains. Problems only stimulate them—the impossible takes a little longer, but not much. They are the most independent of all the types, sometimes to the point of being stubborn. They place a high value on competence—their own and others'.

INTJs often value and use confidently their intuitive insights in fields such as science, engineering, invention, politics, or philosophy. The boldness of their intuition may be of immense value in any field, and should not be smothered in a routine job.

Janice Kofoed, president of catalog sales and direct marketing, agrees that she's an "ENTP" (Extraverted Intuition with Thinking):

People with ENTP preferences are ingenious innovators who always see new possibilities and new ways of doing things. They have a lot of imagination and initiative for starting projects and a lot of impulsive energy for carrying them out. They are sure of the worth of their inspirations and tireless with the problems involved. They are stimulated by difficulties and most ingenious in solving them. They enjoy feeling competent in a variety of areas and value this in others as well.

ENTPs are not likely to stay in any occupation that does not provide many new challenges. With talent, they can be inventors, scientists, journalists, troubleshooters, marketers, promoters, computer analysts, or almost anything that it interests them to be.

Stephen Ferreira, president of film and video production, follows the pattern of an "ENFP" (Extraverted Intuition with Feelings):

People with ENFP preferences can get so interested in their newest project that they have time for little else. Their energy comes from a succession of new enthusiasms and their world is full of possible projects. Their enthusiasm gets other people interested, too. They see so many possible projects that they sometimes have difficulty picking those with the greatest potential.

The ENFPs feeling preference shows in a concern for people. They are skillful in handling people and often have remarkable insight into the possiblities and development of others. They are much drawn to counseling, and can be inspired and inspiring teachers, particularly where they have freedom to innovate. With talent, they can succeed in almost any field that captures their interest—art, journalism, science, advertising, sales, the ministry, or writing, for example.

Lisa Harshaw, president of book publishing, finds herself amazed at the accuracy of her typing as an "INFP" (Introverted Feeling with Intuition):

People with INFP preferences have a great deal of warmth, but may not show it until they know a person well. They are very faithful to duties and obligations related to ideas or people they care about. They take a very personal approach to life, judging everything by their inner ideals and personal values. They stick to their ideals with passionate conviction.

INFPs are curious about new ideas and tend to have insight and long-range vision. Many are interested in books and language and are likely to have a gift of expression; with talent they may be excellent writers. They can be ingenious and persuasive on the subject of their enthusiasms, which are quiet but deep-rooted. They are often attracted to counseling, teaching, literature, art, science, or psychology.

After reviewing the assessments, you conduct a meeting with your seven division presidents, during which a lively discussion ensues about the striking differences among FaraCom's senior management team. Each division president shares his or her own thoughts and feelings about the assessment, and each seems quite comfortable with the results.

Given the professional nature of the assessment process, all seven division presidents seem genuinely excited about how the results will help them improve their decision making and productivity. What happens next astounds you. The division presidents begin talking openly about their strengths and weaknesses. Sean Cope recognizes that his greatest strength lies in promptly responding to a crisis by accurately determining exactly how things really stand at the moment. However, he recognizes his weakness for long-term strategic planning and conceptual thinking about the entire context of cable television operations. He admits that to increase the productivity of his division, he may need some help in this regard. Mona Sork and Alan Peay, responsible for retail operations and magazine publishing, both recognize that their high aptitude for organization, structure, hierarchy, and getting things done on time and within budget represents a great strength to FaraCom, but they also understand that they do not do well enough when it comes to taking advantage of developments in the industry that offer greater growth for their divisions. They welcome more futuristic flexible thinking they can apply to their operations. David Zollweg, responsible for software and CD-ROM publishing, recognizes his ability to create a comprehensive strategic vision for his division, but he also appreciates his inability to take into account the needs and feelings of his people. Janice Kofoed, head of catalog sales and direct marketing, knows she is highly inventive and can easily grasp the larger picture of how the industry will develop, but she admits her weaknesses with regard to implementing her ideas with day-to-day operational systems. Both Zollweg and Kofoed welcome input from Mona Sork and Alan Peay. Stephen Ferreira, responsible for film and video production, values the strength of his opportunistic intuition for identifying new projects, but he also recognizes his weakness in establishing the necessary consistency to keep people on track and performing at high levels with clear standards. Lisa Harshaw, head of book publishing, admits her passion as her greatest strength, but she also laments her unwillingness to pay attention to details outside her areas of impassioned interest. By the end of the session, all welcome more interchange with each other, and they commit themselves to paying more attention to their areas of weakness.

In the following months, the seven division presidents, with your assistance, develop plans for improving their own productivity by maximizing their strengths and minimizing their weaknesses through interaction with one another and with a full deployment of capabilities and talents in their own teams. Many of them reassign individuals in their management teams to take greater advantage of key strengths and to bring about a better blending of capabilities. Their new understanding of psychological type has, it appears, truly built greater productivity throughout FaraCom. Lisa Harshaw sums it up nicely: "I have never felt more comfortable identifying people's strengths and weaknesses. I've also never had a more solid basis for suggesting how people can improve their productivity. MBTI has become a new passion for me."

By the end of your first year as CEO, sales reach $620 million and profits hit break-even, as shown below:

Selected Financial and Productivity Information
(Revenues and Profits in $ Millions)

	First Year	*Previous Year*
Revenues	$622	$508
Profits	$.1	($22)
Employees	1,636	1,612
Revenues per Employee (Actual $)	$380,196	$315,136
Profits per Employee (Actual $)	$61	($13,648)

While the productivity of people in the divisions has increased, you begin your second year as CEO of FaraCom wondering whether you should reassign some of your seven division presidents to better match their strengths and weaknesses with the needs of each business area. For instance, you consider making a shift in assignments between Janice Kofoed, president of catalog sales and direct marketing, and Sean Cope, president of cable television operations. Janice has already created the architecture for catalog sales and direct marketing and seems ready for another challenge, whereas Sean Cope might do a great job implementing Janice's architecture and framework. It also occurs to you that Sean Cope may be perfect for catalogue sales and direct marketing, while Janice Kofoed could do wonders for cable television operations.

And, how about switching roles with Lisa Harshaw, president of book publishing, and Alan Peay, president of magazine publishing? Peay, as an ISTJ, has created a very structured and organized operation in magazine publishing, but the division lacks conceptual life and future orientation, particularly in terms of new publications. On the other hand, Lisa Harshaw has created a vibrant visionary culture in book publishing, but she needs more follow up on mundane operational details. You believe that a shift between these two could take full advantage of Alan Peay's penchant for organization and Lisa Harshaw's skill at impassioned culture building.

For the moment, you feel that Mona Sork should remain in charge of retail operations, which need a lot of operational systemization and structure, and you think David Zollweg should stay put in software and CD-ROM publishing, where a good conceptual logician might most easily find the right vision and plan for the future. Also, you see a perfect match between Stephen Ferreira and film and video production. His insightful opportunism will continue to discover film and video projects that meet the needs of FaraCom customers. When you discuss the potential changes with your seven division presidents, both individually and as a group, you encounter some initial resistance, but the four division presidents involved in switching eventually agree to make the moves. You keep your fingers crossed.

Over the next several months, the new assignments seem to work out beautifully as FaraCom continues to grow and productivity reaches new heights. By the end of your second year as CEO, sales reach $750 million and profits continue to build, as shown below:

Selected Financial and Productivity Information
(Revenues and Profits in $ Millions)

	Second Year	First Year
Revenues	$748	$622
Profits	$10	$.1
Employees	1,865	1,636
Revenues per Employee (Actual $)	$401,072	$380,196
Profits per Employee (Actual $)	$5,362	$61

Although Bill Faragut expresses satisfaction with your performance, he recommends a companywide productivity assessment as a precursor for the next round of improvement. You agree with Faragut's request even though you suspect he's just trying to keep your feet to the fire. Remembering that Faragut seemed suspicious of your emphasis on psychological type when you began it, you wonder whether he's changed his mind. Regardless, you're confident that FaraCom's performance will speak for itself.

To learn about the results of the companywide productivity assessment, turn to Chapter 14, page 65.

CHAPTER 10

Hiring an Outside Consultant

Impressed by the book *The Fourth Dimension,* written by four former Ernst & Young consultants, Angus, Berrett, Bott, and Hickman, you decide to hire two of the authors, Marlon Berrett and Craig Bott, to help you assess the productivity of your seven division presidents in three dimensions of work outlined in *The Fourth Dimension:* PowerWork, NetWork, and ValueWork. PowerWork relates to doing the right things, and doing them right, an action-oriented dimension that strives for effectiveness and efficiency. NetWork deals with developing skills and relationships in ways that bring meaning, purpose, and fulfillment to people's lives. ValueWork means providing the greatest value to the greatest number of people, the thinking and discovery dimension of work. The fourth dimension, MetaWork, involves consistently working in and orchestrating the work of others in all three dimensions.

As you study the three dimensions of work, and with the help of consultants Berrett and Bott, you learn that each of your seven division presidents works differently in each dimension. Sean Cope, president of cable television operations, Mona Sork, president of retail operations, and Alan Peay, president of magazine publishing, all seem fully engaged in PowerWork. They constantly stress efficiency and effectiveness while keeping their eyes fixed on results. However, you see a need in all three for improving NetWorking and ValueWorking. On the other hand, David Zollweg, president of software and CD-ROM publishing, and Janice Kofoed, president of catalog sales and direct marketing, seem naturally gifted at ValueWork, always trying to find what will deliver the greatest value to the greatest number of FaraCom customers. They are always toiling to better understand the wants and needs of their customers and then working hard to creatively meet and surpass their customers' expectations. However, you wonder whether Zollweg and Kofoed pay enough attention to PowerWorking and NetWorking. Finally, Stephen Ferreira, president of film and video production, and Lisa Harshaw, president of book publishing, both demonstrate high commitment and devotion to NetWorking, which manifests itself in the strong people-oriented cultures of the film and book divisions. They are always building unity and common purpose into their organizations. However, you also realize that they need to pay more attention to PowerWorking and ValueWorking.

As you think about your people's strengths and weaknesses in the three fields of the MetaWork System, you see that their work stems a good deal from their natural preferences and orientations. If you're going to make FaraCom the most productive company in the country or in the world, you must help your seven division presidents operate more fully in all dimensions. It won't be easy getting everyone up to speed in all three dimensions because their natural strengths, weaknesses, and patterns of preferences will not easily change. After a lot of soul searching on this issue, you decide to embark on a series of retreats designed to allow your division presidents to examine more thoroughly how each performs in the three dimensions of work and to discuss ways to enhance everyone's performance in all three.

Over the next several months, you, the two outside consultants, and your seven division presidents become intimately acquainted with one another's strengths, weaknesses, orientations, and preferences. Even though many of the discussions prove grueling and difficult, you begin to see progress as the division presidents come to recognize and evaluate their work on a daily basis in each of the three dimensions. By the end of the year, your senior team has attained a much keener awareness of their work habits, which has resulted in improved productivity companywide. Sales climb to over $600 million and profits break into the black, as shown by the following:

Selected Financial and Productivity Information
(Revenues and Profits in $ Millions)

	First Year	*Previous Year*
Revenues	$609	$508
Profits	$2	($22)
Employees	1,651	1,612
Revenues per Employee (Actual $)	$368,867	$315,136
Profits per Employee (Actual $)	$1,211	($13,648)

During your second year as CEO, you help each of your division presidents work out a customized program for achieving greater improvement in their own productivity and the productivity of their management teams. They proceed to do so on a dual course: (1) continuing improvements in their own productivity by spending more time and affording more attention to those work dimensions outside their natural affinity, and (2) increasing the awareness and understanding of their teams with respect to the three fields or dimensions of the MetaWork System, much as you did for them last year.

Slowly but surely, you find your seven division presidents transforming their divisions as they teach the three fields of work to their management teams, making more people more sensitive to working in all three. Productivity increases among your senior team and among the management teams in each of the seven divisions helping to push the company to $725 million in sales and $30 million in profits by the end of your second year as CEO, as shown below:

Selected Financial and Productivity Information
(Revenues and Profits in $ Millions)

	Second Year	*First Year*
Revenues	$725	$609
Profits	$30	$2
Employees	1,817	1,651
Revenues per Employee (Actual $)	$399,009	$368,867
Profits per Employee (Actual $)	$16,511	$1,211

After the first of the year, Bill Faragut asks for a companywide assessment of productivity, and while you wonder about his true motives, you agree because you believe that the assessment will prove the success of your productivity improvement efforts. Although Faragut tells you he merely wants to assess the exact extent of FaraCom's productivity improvements, you suspect that he really wants a check on your own performance as CEO. Still, you look forward to the opportunity to see, in more precise terms, the impact of the MetaWork System on the company's performance. The companywide assessment of productivity will, you assume, provide the perfect launching pad for further improvements in the future.

To find out how FaraCom fares with the productivity assessment, turn to Chapter 14, page 65.

CHAPTER 11

Adopting Franklin's Time-Management Program

As you meet with your seven division presidents to discuss your decision to focus on companywide time management, you promote Franklin's Day Planner system by citing several testimonials from individuals who have used it to increase productivity. From an account executive at Merrill Lynch: "I can't express the feelings of accomplishment that I have from using the system. My production has increased, I am able to go on more appointments, and I seem to have more time for my family. My Day Planner is fantastic and I use it to its full capacity." From a middle manager at Dow Chemical: "The Day Planner is fantastic! I am now totally dependent on it." From a professional at Price Waterhouse, "Probably the best management/personal development course ever taken and one I'll highly recommend to business associates and friends." From a manager at Bank of America: "I enjoyed the seminar very much and find it exciting to actually be organized. It seems that I am able to get much more done with considerably less effort."

You also present two options for FaraCom's own adoption of the system: a half-day or full-day seminar. After some discussion, the seven division presidents vote for the half-day seminar and seem genuinely excited about the prospect of learning how the Day Planner system might instill more effective time management throughout the organization. The half-day seminar will include an introduction to the natural laws that maximize effectiveness and the basic idea that event control provides the key to time management; a thorough discussion of event control; planning as a key to control; the ordering and prioritizing of events; a look at the productivity pyramid (identifying values, establishing long-range goals, setting immediate objectives); and, finally, the use of the Franklin Day Planner on a daily basis.

To set the stage for a companywide roll-out, you decide that you and the seven division presidents should take the seminar first in order to determine any customization it may need before all of FaraCom's 1,600 employees take it. Within a month, you and your seven division presidents attend a seminar with a Franklin Day Planner presenter, who tells you, "Everyone feels the need to gain more control of his or her time, but few actually achieve this goal." The seminar leader adds, "People's effort to do so often gets lost in mechanics—keeping lists, making notes, following tips on doing things right. However, this seminar, which has been taught to hundreds of thousands of the nation's most successful executives and professionals, concentrates on the question of doing the right things. It teaches the art of focusing your time on activities that make the most sense for you, in light of your values and long-range goals."

Throughout the morning, you learn why effective time management does not stem from watching the clock—the secret lies in controlling events, not hours. You also learn about the interrelationship between event control, self-esteem, and productivity, which combine to lay the foundation for increased effectiveness.

By the end of the seminar, each of you take away your own Franklin Day Planner with a three-month supply of pages for daily planning. You and your division presidents commit yourselves to testing it for a 30-day period before launching the seminar companywide. At the end of 30 days, your division presidents feel that they have improved their productivity by using the Franklin Day Planner, and some feel highly enthusiastic, namely Sean Cope, president of cable television operations, Mona Sork, president of retail operations, and Alan Peay, president of magazine publishing. While Sean Cope still rebels against the whole idea of trying to control events, he recognizes the program as an important way to gain greater control of his schedule, "I know the Planner has decreased the amount of wasted time in my schedule." Mona Sork and Alan Peay consider the Day Planner as the perfect way to gain greater productivity. Alan comments, "Everyone in the company needs this tool." The four other presidents—David Zollweg, president of software and CD-ROM publishing, Janice Kofoed, president of catalog sales and direct marketing, Stephen Ferreira, president of film and video production, and Lisa Harshaw, president of book publishing—like the program well enough, but remain somewhat skeptical that it will increase overall productivity in any major way. Janice Kofoed sums up their feelings,

"The Planner will help, but I don't think we should expect it to solve all our problems."

After talks with each of the four lukewarm division presidents, you convince them that they have nothing to lose by adopting the Franklin Day Planner in their divisions. Though they all agree to proceed with the Franklin system companywide, David Zollweg and Janice Kofoed make it clear to you that they think their people must eventually do much more than manage time more effectively to increase long-term productivity. You agree with that view, but hope that more experience with the Franklin Day Planner will accomplish more than they imagine. You remain hopeful that as people master the Franklin Day Planner system, the results will turn these four division presidents into fans of the system.

By year end, almost half of FaraCom's 1,700 employees complete the Franklin seminar. Sales increase to $576 million and profits move toward break-even as shown below:

Selected Financial and Productivity Information
(Revenues and Profits in $ Millions)

	First Year	*Previous Year*
Revenues	$576	$508
Profits	($4)	($22)
Employees	1,694	1,612
Revenues per Employee (Actual $)	$340,024	$315,136
Profits per Employee (Actual $)	$2,361	($13,648)

During the first quarter of your second year as CEO, the rest of the FaraCom employees attend the Franklin seminar and begin using their Day Planners in their everyday work. With its set of customized personal binders, forms, tabs, and accessories, the Franklin Day Planner becomes a staple instrument for controlling events throughout the FaraCom organization during your second year as CEO. By year end, you're delighted when all seven of your division presidents admit that productivity has increased in each of their divisions.

As you reflect back over the last two years as CEO of FaraCom, you feel pleased with the results of your emphasis on time management and believe that the company will continue to grow and increase its productivity. However, some of your division presidents believe that the company should go even further in its efforts to enhance productivity. As David Zollweg insists, "All productivity increases through the use of the Franklin Day Planner will peak next year. Then what do we do?"

As the year ends, sales climb to $669 million, with profits moving into the black, as shown below:

Selected Financial and Productivity Information
(Revenues and Profits in $ Millions)

	First Year	*Previous Year*
Revenues	$669	$576
Profits	$4	($4)
Employees	1,827	1,694
Revenues per Employee (Actual $)	$366,174	$340,024
Profits per Employee (Actual $)	$2,189	($2,361)

After the first of the year, Bill Faragut tells you that despite this progress he wants to conduct a companywide assessment of productivity. You wonder whether some of the division presidents have communicated to him their concern that the Franklin Day Planner will not deliver sufficient further improvements in productivity, or that they feel disappointed in the level of productivity improvements to date. Although somewhat skeptical of Faragut's true motive behind this productivity assessment, you agree to it and hope that it will support your decisions over the past two years.

To find out how FaraCom fares in the companywide productivity assessment, turn to Chapter 14, page 65.

CHAPTER 12

Implementing Covey's "First Things First" Philosophy

Convinced that productivity at FaraCom will increase only when employees learn to base their actions on principles rather than on procedures, you buy copies of Stephen Covey's new book, *First Things First,* for each of your seven division presidents and ask them to review it before your next management meeting. Having been impressed by Covey's earlier book, *The Seven Habits of Highly Effective People,* you believe that *First Things First* could help employees learn to make decisions and take action based on principle rather than on procedure.

At the management meeting with your seven division presidents, you review Covey's concept of "true north" principles as the absolutes that should guide employees and organizations. You quote directly from Covey's book: "What is north? Is it a matter of opinion? Is it something we should vote on? Is it subject to the democratic process? No, because north is a reality that is independent of us. The reality of true north gives context and meaning to where we are, where we want to go, and how to get there. Without a compass or stars or a correct understanding of our location, we may have trouble locating it, but it's always there. Just as real as true north in the physical world are the timeless laws of cause and effect that operate in the world of personal effectiveness and human interaction. The collective wisdom of the ages reveals these principles as recurring themes, foundational to every truly great person or society . . . What we are talking about are the true north realities upon which quality of life is based. These principles deal with things that, in the long run, will create happiness and quality of life results. They include principles such as service and reciprocity. They deal with the processes of growth and change. They include the laws that govern effective fulfillment of basic human needs and capacities." To drive home this point, you then tell your seven division presidents that Louis Gerstner, CEO of IBM, admits to struggling with one major issue as he works to alter the culture at IBM: to help people act on such principles rather than on procedure or practice or process. "That's what we need at FaraCom," you conclude.

After additional discussion of the concepts contained in *First Things First,* you find that your seven division presidents fully agree with Covey's ideas and think his daily planning system based on principles could, in fact, improve productivity companywide. With this senior team consensus in place, you move forward over the next several weeks, exploring the Covey planning system's distinction between tasks that are important but not urgent and those that are not important, but urgent. Focusing on important but not urgent tasks allows for appropriate preparation, prevention, values clarification, planning, relationship building, and empowerment. You also explore the Covey system's identification of different roles, such as manager, father or mother, community leader, project leader. After completing an extensive review of *First Things First,* you decide to hire members of the Covey Leadership organization to help design a companywide application of the Covey planning system.

In succeeding months, FaraCom institutes a daily planning system throughout the organization, and by the end of the year, every employee has begun using it. By year end, sales reach $600 million, with profits surpassing break-even, as shown below:

Selected Financial and Productivity Information
(Revenues and Profits in $ Millions)

	First Year	*Previous Year*
Revenues	$601	$508
Profits	$3	($22)
Employees	1,714	1,612
Revenues per Employee (Actual $)	$350,642	$315,136
Profits per Employee (Actual $)	$1,750	($13,648)

During your second year as FaraCom's CEO, you work hard to internalize all aspects of the Covey planning system into the company's culture, always stressing the importance of principles as the driving force for action and decision making. You work with your seven division presidents to identify the principles that should guide each of their divisions in the quest for success, identifying specific ones for each division, such as programming for the cable television operations division, product variety for retail operations, niche readership for magazine publishing, topic selection for software and CD-ROM publishing, list development for catalog sales and direct marketing, script acquisition for film and video production, and author selection for book publishing. In addition to these division-specific principles, companywide principles dealing with service, customer satisfaction, employee fulfillment, and open and candid communications begin forming the bedrock of principles for FaraCom.

Over the ensuing months, the focus on principles breathes new life into the organization, and productivity jumps as people use the Covey planning system to focus on the principles that should guide decisions with respect to their own personal lives, their divisions, and the whole company. By the end of your second year as CEO, sales reach $710 million and profits hit $26 million, as shown below:

Selected Financial and Productivity Information
(Revenues and Profits in $ Millions)

	Second Year	First Year
Revenues	$710	$601
Profits	$26	$3
Employees	1,812	1,714
Revenues per Employee (Actual $)	$391,832	$350,642
Profits per Employee (Actual $)	$14,349	$1,750

Despite this performance, Bill Faragut, chairman of the board, informs you that he'd like to conduct a companywide productivity assessment to determine precisely how far FaraCom has progressed during your two years of leadership. You welcome the assessment because you feel it will prove the wisdom of your past choices and provide an important benchmark for future progress.

To find out how FaraCom stacks up in the companywide productivity assessment, turn to Chapter 14, page 65.

CHAPTER 13

Installing EmpowerTech's Improvement System

Since you believe that technology will produce the greatest increases in productivity over the next few years, you select the EmpowerTech system, which promises to maximize communication, integrate decision making, and stimulate individual performance. EmpowerTech's system centers around a phone-fax-computer for every employee and includes proprietary software that integrates goal setting, decision making, and performance evaluation throughout a company. In essence, it connects every employee to every other employee through E-mail, fax, and phone. The architecture of the daily planning system within the EmpowerTech framework allows for immediate evaluation of proposed decisions or anticipated actions through a congruency test based on the overall strategic goals and objectives of the company. Every employee can thus determine, at any given moment, whether a decision, action, or plan matches the company's overall goals and objectives. The system also produces quick financial assessments of projects and communicates those figures to the senior team, making it much easier for people to get their decisions evaluated, approved, or rejected for the right reasons. Adopting EmpowerTech's system will require a major investment of money and time, but you've convinced Bill Faragut that the results will far outweigh the $15 million price tag.

You spend the next several months laying the groundwork for the system and putting every employee through the necessary training. David Zollweg, president of software and CD-ROM publishing, loves the EmpowerTech system because of the frameworking and conceptualizing capabilities. In his own words, he expresses, "I've never used a program

61

that so easily links everything I'm concerned about into one integrated picture. It's going to eliminate a lot of wasted time and energy from my work life."

On the other hand, Sean Cope, president of cable television operations, hates the system because he does not see the practical benefits. He says, "I can see my people spending a lot of time figuring out how their jobs and assignments fit into the overall scheme of things and never getting their work done."

Regardless of the wide range of initial reactions to the EmpowerTech system, you press forward with confidence. By year end, sales reach $580 million and profits improve slightly, as shown below:

Selected Financial and Productivity Information
(Revenues and Profits in $ Millions)

	First Year	Previous Year
Revenues	$579	$508
Profits	($17)	($22)
Employees	1,809	1,612
Revenues per Employee (Actual $)	$320,066	$315,136
Profits per Employee (Actual $)	($9,397)	($13,648)

Though marginal, these increases and the promise of increased productivity in the coming year seem to satisfy Bill Faragut. The EmpowerTech system comes fully on-line at the beginning of your second year as CEO, and employees throughout the company respond enthusiastically to this opportunity to increase their productivity. Luckily, the extensive EmpowerTech training and preparation have broken down most of the resistance to such a comprehensive new system.

During the next several months, you see clear progress in each division as employees work hard to maximize their productivity. David Zollweg, president of software and CD-ROM publishing, comments, "There's more coordination within and across divisions than I ever dreamed possible." Unfortunately, Sean Cope, president of cable television operations, still clings to his old way of doing things, but he has started using the E-mail and performance-appraisal dimensions of the system. Reluctantly, he admits, "The system does start to grow on you after awhile."

As decision making throughout the organization becomes simpler and more streamlined, people no longer complain about red tape and bureaucracy getting in their way. Information from employees throughout the company about strategic developments or customer feedback finds its way into the system quickly, empowering the eyes and ears of the FaraCom organization. In one case, Lisa Harshaw, president of book publishing, discovered an odd pattern of book sales for a recently published book that would have taken her weeks or months to identify without EmpowerTech. In response, she immediately targeted the hot spots—Seattle, St. Louis, Tampa, and Houston—for intensified publicity and sales efforts. As a result, book sales doubled initial projections within the first six months.

Productivity grows, and sales in each of the divisions reaches new highs by the end of your second year as CEO. Sales increase to $680 million, with profits reaching $8 million, as shown below:

Selected Financial and Productivity Information
(Revenues and Profits in $ Millions)

	Second Year	First Year
Revenues	$681	$579
Profits	$8	($17)
Employees	1,845	1,809
Revenues per Employee (Actual $)	$369,106	$320,066
Profits per Employee (Actual $)	$4,336	($9,397)

After the first of the year, however, Bill Faragut tells you he wants to see a comprehensive measure of the productivity increase at FaraCom and insists you conduct a companywide productivity assessment. You quickly agree, knowing that the results will prove the wisdom of your decision to adopt the EmpowerTech system.

To discover how FaraCom fares in the companywide productivity assessment, turn to Chapter 14, page 65.

CHAPTER 14

Dealing with an Outside Assessment of FaraCom's Productivity

Bill Faragut has recommended that Ernst & Young perform the company-wide productivity assessment, which the consultants will base on three major measurements: value-added per employee, comparison to "best in world" competitors, and FaraCom's own past versus-present productivity improvements. The value-added measure subtracts the total dollar cost of all materials purchased from the total dollar revenues of products and services sold to obtain a total dollar value-added figure, divided by the total number of FaraCom employees, resulting in a value-added per employee measurement. Two years ago, the value-added figure per employee hovered around $100,000.

The comparison to "best in world" competitors measure averages the published sales per employee, profits per employee, and other available data from ten highly successful communications and entertainment companies with operations similar in whole or part to FaraCom's. The combined data results in a "best in world" comparison index of 1,000, to which similar FaraCom data can be compared.

The internal FaraCom Productivity Index measures improvement in a variety of areas, such as quality, errors, output, rework, and resources utilized. A composite number of "100" represents the baseline (the point just before you assumed your current job). The original Ernst & Young consulting engagement, of which you had been a part, established that benchmark.

At this stage of *The Productivity Game*, you will pause to assess not only the productivity of FaraCom based on the choices you have already

65

made, but the outcomes of choices you did not make as well. Based on the first two decisions in the game, you could have produced one of nine different outcomes, all of which you can now review and rank. The table that follows identifies the choices in your first and second decisions.

First Decision	Second Decision	
Chapter 2 Maximizing Your Own Productivity	Chapter 5	Creating an Integrated Strategy and Theme
	Chapter 6	Developing Strong Divisional Strategies and Cultures
	Chapter 7	Training Your Seven Division Presidents to Think Strategically
Chapter 3 Increasing the Productivity of Division Presidents	Chapter 8	Allowing the Seven Division Presidents to Set Their Own Agendas
	Chapter 9	Identifying the Psychological Type of Each Division President
	Chapter 10	Hiring an Outside Consultant
Chapter 4 Building Productivity Throughout the Entire Organization	Chapter 11	Adopting Franklin's Time Management Program
	Chapter 12	Implementing Covey's "First Things First" Philosophy
	Chapter 13	Installing EmpowerTech's Improvement System

To review and compare each of the nine possible productivity outcomes so far (Chapters 5 through 13), review the following:

Chapter 5, Creating an Integrated Strategy and Theme—If you have chosen to deploy yourself and your own capabilities toward developing an integrated strategy and theme, drawing upon strategic synergy and coordination to increase productivity, you achieve the following productivity improvements:

	Assessment	Benchmark
Value-Added Index	$112,000	$100,000
"Best in World" Comparison Index	632	1,000
FaraCom Productivity Index	110	100

Chapter 6, Developing Strong Divisional Strategies and Cultures—If you decided to deploy yourself and your own capabilities and expertise by developing strong strategies and cultures in each of the divisions, you achieve the following outcome:

	Assessment	Benchmark
Value-Added Index	$124,000	$100,000
"Best in World" Comparison Index	743	1,000
FaraCom Productivity Index	121	100

Chapter 7, Training Your Seven Division Presidents to Think Strategically—If you deploy yourself with an eye to personally training each of your seven division presidents in strategic thinking, the following outcome occurs:

	Assessment	Benchmark
Value-Added Index	$109,000	$100,000
"Best in World" Comparison Index	581	1,000
FaraCom Productivity Index	106	100

Chapter 8, Allowing the Seven Division Presidents to Set Their Own Agendas—If you focused on building the productivity of your seven division presidents by allowing them to set their own agendas for increasing productivity, the following results:

	Assessment	Benchmark
Value-Added Index	$110,000	$100,000
"Best in World" Comparison Index	607	1,000
FaraCom Productivity Index	108	100

Chapter 9, Identifying the Psychological Type of Each Division President—If focusing on the productivity of the seven division presidents caused you to assess each of their personality types in an effort to develop a customized productivity improvement program for each one, you achieve the following:

	Assessment	Benchmark
Value-Added Index	$126,000	$100,000
"Best in World" Comparison Index	808	1,000
FaraCom Productivity Index	133	100

Chapter 10, Hiring an Outside Consultant—If you focused on building the productivity of the seven division presidents by hiring an outside consultant, you achieve the following outcome:

	Assessment	Benchmark
Value-Added Index	$136,000	$100,000
"Best in World" Comparison Index	832	1,000
FaraCom Productivity Index	139	100

Chapter 11, Adopting Franklin's Time Management Program—By focusing on building productivity in the entire organization and using the Franklin Day Planner as the major vehicle for achieving productivity improvements, you capture the following results:

	Assessment	Benchmark
Value-Added Index	$119,000	$100,000
"Best in World" Comparison Index	701	1,000
FaraCom Productivity Index	118	100

Chapter 12, Implementing Covey's "First Things First" Philosophy— If you focused on building productivity companywide by embracing the Covey Leadership Center's "First Things First" daily planning system, you get to this point:

	Assessment	Benchmark
Value-Added Index	$135,000	$100,000
"Best in World" Comparison Index	836	1,000
FaraCom Productivity Index	138	100

Chapter 13, Installing EmpowerTech's Improvement System—If you chose to embrace the high-tech system fueled by EmpowerTech's productivity software as a means to building productivity companywide, you reach the following:

	Assessment	Benchmark
Value-Added Index	$115,000	$100,000
"Best in World" Comparison Index	735	1,000
FaraCom Productivity Index	119	100

The following table summarizes the performance and productivity outcomes of the nine different tracks so far in the game:

Chapter	Sales	Profits	Employees	Sales per Employee	Profit per Employee	Value-Added Index	"Best in World" Index	FaraCom Index	Composite Ranking
5	$620	$2	1,718	$360,885	$1,164	$112,000	632	110	7
6	$702	$10	1,875	$374,400	$5,333	$124,000	743	121	4
7	$598	$(5)	1,842	$324,647	$(2,714)	$109,000	581	106	9
8	$602	$(2)	1,709	$352,253	$(1,170)	$110,000	607	108	8
9	$748	$10	1,865	$401,072	$5,362	$126,000	808	133	3
10	$725	$30	1,817	$399,009	$16,511	$136,000	832	139	1
11	$669	$4	1,827	$366,174	$2,189	$119,000	701	118	6
12	$710	$26	1,812	$391,832	$14,349	$135,000	836	138	2
13	$681	$8	1,845	$369,106	$4,336	$115,000	735	119	5
Benchmark						$100,000	1,000	100	—

Now that you've had a chance to review the nine possible outcomes so far, you can shift, if you desire, to another decision-making track based on these interim outcomes. If, however, you feel strongly committed to the course that you have already pursued, you may want to stick with it, because the ranking of outcomes at this point in FaraCom's development will probably change in succeeding years. On the other hand, if you have developed any insecurity or concern about the choices you have made to date, you can immediately move to another decision-making track. Which road will you choose: the one you have been traveling, or one not taken?

If you choose to shift to or remain with the decision making that put you into Chapter 5, Creating an Integrated Strategy and Theme, turn to Chapter 15, page 73.

If you wish to stick with or shift to the outcome in Chapter 6, Developing Strong Divisional Strategies and Cultures in each of the divisions, turn to Chapter 16, page 75.

If you decide to change to or hold to the outcome in Chapter 7, Training Your Seven Presidents to Think Strategically, turn to Chapter 17, page 77.

If you want to move to or stay with Chapter 8, allowing the seven division presidents to set their own productivity improvement agendas, turn to Chapter 18, page 79.

If you prefer shifting to or remaining with the outcome in Chapter 9, identifying the psychological type of each division president, turn to Chapter 19, page 83.

If you would like to move to or hold to the outcome in Chapter 10, hiring an outside consultant, turn to Chapter 20, page 87.

If you like the idea of staying with or moving to the outcome of Chapter 11, adopting Franklin's Time Management Program, turn to Chapter 21, page 91.

If you desire to change to or stick with the outcome in Chapter 12, implementing Covey's "First Things First" philosophy, turn to Chapter 22, page 93.

If you would rather shift to or hold to Chapter 13's outcome, installing EmpowerTech's productivity improvement system, turn to Chapter 23, page 97.

Note: If you decide to shift to a different outcome, you may want to review the previous two chapters that led to the outcome you're choosing. To do so, consult the table of first and second decisions at the beginning of this chapter.

CHAPTER 15

Refining a Companywide Strategy and Theme

Under increasing pressure from Bill Faragut to quickly increase productivity, you continue building on your efforts to develop a values-based strategy and theme throughout FaraCom by overseeing each division president's efforts to strengthen their organizational cultures and base their strategic decisions on values. Janice Kofoed, president of catalog sales and direct marketing, proves the power of the strategic theme when she offers each of the other divisions the opportunity to tap her division's growing family entertainment values-based marketing list for distribution of their products. Kofoed's operation grows rapidly during your third year as CEO by tapping into this previously underserved market. The new values-based orientation especially benefits the film and video production division, under Stephen Ferreira's leadership, software and CD-ROM publishing, under David Zollweg, and cable television operations, under Sean Cope, although the retail operations, magazine publishing, and book publishing lag behind.

By midyear, you decide to close down retail operations, not through liquidation, but by selling off the retail stores to a group of interested buyers. Mona Sork decides to leave FaraCom in order to remain in the retail field, and within a few months you conclude the deal, fully removing FaraCom from the retailing business. As you had hoped, book publishing and magazine publishing slowly but surely begin to tap into the demand for values-based literature in book and magazine forms.

Alan Peay launches a new magazine called *Family First,* which gets off to a slow start, but seems to promise great potential in the future. Lisa Harshaw works with a group of professors from Notre Dame, Brigham Young

73

University, SMU, and Yale to launch a values-based literature series that includes reprints of classics, as well as new works. The first huge success in the series comes from an anthology of stories entitled *The Book of Values*, which outsells the best-selling book that inspired it, William Bennett's *The Book of Virtues*. As the series grows, it provides a framework to guide students and parents in selecting values-based literature. The series appeals to the direct-marketing division, which easily identifies customers who want to sign up for the entire series, much as they would in a book club. Harshaw even proposes creating a new book club division for the company.

You continue to work hard to develop business processes that more fully coordinate and unify FaraCom's divisions around the values-based strategic theme. Drawing on total quality and learning organization ideas, you tie everything that happens within FaraCom to the values-based vision. While the company has failed to show huge productivity improvements after your first two years as CEO, performance jumps at the end of your third year, as shown in the accompanying table.

Selected Financial and Productivity Information
(Revenues and Profits in $ Millions)

	Third Year	*Second Year*
Revenues	$760	$620
Profits	$31	$2
Employees	1,876	1,718
Revenues per Employee (Actual $)	$405,117	$360,885
Profits per Employee (Actual $)	$16,524	$1,164

Not surprisingly, Bill Faragut requests another companywide productivity assessment to measure the improvements.

To discover the results of FaraCom's second productivity assessment, turn to Chapter 24, page 101.

CHAPTER 16

Continuing to Develop Strong Divisional Strategies and Cultures

Under great pressure to increase productivity in each of the divisions, particularly after the recent companywide assessment revealed fairly mediocre performance, you assure Bill Faragut that the groundwork you've so carefully laid in each of the divisions will now begin paying off in a big way. By now you know each of the operations intimately, and you have successfully helped each of them develop a sound strategy and a strong culture. In what many will later call a brilliant move, you propose to Bill Faragut and the FaraCom board of directors that the company spin out each of the seven divisions as separate entities, with public stock offerings. You argue that all of the divisional strategies and cultures differ so distinctly and have instilled such a deep sense of ownership among the separate management teams that the spin-offs will allow them to exploit fully their individual plans for growth through internal development and external acquisitions.

The plan you propose emulates ThermoElectron's spin-out strategy, whereby the company offers 60 percent of a division's stock to the public, while retaining 40 percent for itself. Your modification of that strategy divides ownership into thirds, one-third ownership for FaraCom, one third for management, and one third for the public. When the plan receives informal approval from the board, you recommend a formula for strategic development in each division, encouraging each to spend two thirds of its time focusing on internal development and one third on acquisition and external development through mergers, joint ventures, and alliances. You spend one third of your own time managing and overseeing the FaraCom companies, and two thirds developing future spin-out opportunities. You also outline three fundamental tenets for guiding the ongoing strategic development and culture building in all FaraCom companies:

- Innovation Leadership
- Market Niche Dominance
- Radical Improvement

The board officially approves the first two spin-outs, Cable Television Operations and Software & CD-ROM Publishing, for public offerings before the end of your third year as CEO. Productivity across the FaraCom companies and divisions increases dramatically, particularly in the two spin-out divisions. Sales reach $800 million with profits climbing to $29 million, as shown below:

Selected Financial and Productivity Information
(Revenues and Profits in $ Millions)

	Third Year	*Second Year*
Revenues	$802	$702
Profits	$29	$10
Employees	1,909	1,875
Revenues per Employee (Actual $)	$420,115	$374,400
Profits per Employee (Actual $)	$15,191	$5,333

At this point you and Bill Faragut decide to conduct another companywide productivity assessment. That assessment will not only show you how far the company has come, but it should also reveal future opportunities for further development.

To discover the results of this second companywide productivity assessment, turn to Chapter 24, page 101.

CHAPTER 17

Increasing Emphasis on Strategic Thinking

After the companywide productivity assessment, Bill Faragut and the board of directors make it clear that if you cannot dramatically improve productivity in the coming year, they may start looking for another CEO. You remain committed to your emphasis on strategic thinking because you believe that doing so will produce tremendous productivity improvements, but you decide that the time has come to push training further down in each division.

As a first step in that direction, you take functional teams in each division through intensive training and development programs focusing on performance, productivity, strategic thinking, culture building, change management, continuous improvement, organizational learning, and individual leadership-skills development. Emulating companies such as Motorola that have heavily invested in similar training and development, you establish FaraCom University and begin construction of a new facility in Orlando, Florida.

Over the next several months, you personally guide the senior teams and many functional teams from each division through an intensive training session, bringing in experts from all over the country to help strengthen FaraCom's management fabric. Two presenters, Hamel and Prahalad, authors of *The Competitive Future*, had a particular impact on FaraCom executives and managers as they stressed the importance of maintaining intellectual flexibility, foresight, and originality. Most of them went away from the three-day session with a new commitment and plenty of tools to better manage the company's most prized possession: intellectual capital.

You remain convinced that if you devote your personal time and attention to developing strategic thinking among your seven division presidents, their management teams, and the next layer of management, you will build the strongest possible base for FaraCom's future and, in the process, raise productivity and performance to acceptable levels.

By year end, sales do improve to $650 million and profits hit break-even as shown below:

Selected Financial and Productivity Information
(Revenues and Profits in $ Millions)

	Third Year	Second Year
Revenues	$648	$598
Profits	$.2	($5)
Employees	1,963	1,842
Revenues per Employee (Actual $)	$330,107	$324,647
Profits per Employee (Actual $)	$102	($2,714)

With a lot of anecdotal evidence of growth and development among key personnel in each division relating to improved business plans, revised management reports, and more accurate sales projections, you feel satisfied with FaraCom's progress. However, you also feel mounting pressure from Bill Faragut to improve productivity in a clear and measurable way. He tells you, frankly, "I'm not convinced what you're doing will impact productivity or results. It all seems too vague and abstract." Not surprisingly, he asks for another companywide assessment, which you reluctantly accept.

To find out how FaraCom fares in this assessment, turn to Chapter 24, page 101.

CHAPTER 18

Further Encouraging the Seven Division Presidents to Pursue Their Own Productivity Agendas

You still believe that giving your seven division presidents the freedom to follow their own productivity programs in each of their divisions will pay off handsomely in the long term. Since the results so far have not proven spectacular, however, you decide to intensify your relationship with each of the seven division presidents, further encouraging them to design and develop approaches singularly appropriate for their own people and their own businesses. In order to get them thinking about issues of motivation and autonomy, you give them copies of Matthew Fox's new book *The Reinvention of Work*, wherein the controversial author urges readers to overcome "feelings of isolation, insecurity, and alienation" in work by embracing a new vision of work "where the self is not sacrificed for a job, but is sanctified by authentic soul work . . . where intellect, heart, and health come together in a harmony of essential life experiences that celebrates the whole person." As a result, Stephen Ferreira, president of film and video production, and Lisa Harshaw, president of book publishing, discover creative ways to motivate employees by tying compensation to results and giving every employee more freedom in terms of setting schedules and designing work environments.

Janice Kofoed, president of catalog sales and direct marketing, and David Zollweg, president of software and CD-ROM development and publishing, seem so buried in the growth of their businesses that they spend little time worrying about productivity. However, you decide that effectively managing growth should, in fact, improve productivity over time. Once they get beyond the intense development phase, they can turn their attention to further productivity improvements. You worry most about Sean Cope, president of cable television operations, Mona Sork, president of retail operations, and Alan Peay, president of magazine publishing, who seem unable to envision new ways of increasing productivity in their divisions. Although they have been working hard to develop unique customized programs for productivity improvement, as far as you can see they have not really come up with anything new, creative, or insightful.

In an unusual move, you decide to take Cope, Sork, and Peay off site to a retreat, where you can explore new innovations in their productivity programs. While trying to get the three division presidents to look beyond the present by imagining new approaches proves a grueling experience, you do detect some progress as they begin to broaden their horizons and deepen their understanding of a fuller array of options for increasing the productivity of their people. However, you know you've got problems when Mona Sork, president of retail operations, pulls you aside during the retreat and says, "This was a very interesting and enlightening exercise, but I'm not convinced it's going to help make my people more productive. I still think we need more direction and structure from you or an outside consultant to give us a productivity improvement program with real teeth, something tried and proven."

Unfortunately, you realize too late that Sork was right. In the end, you acknowledge that little, if any, improvement in productivity will occur this year in these three divisions. Can the other four pick up the slack while you continue coaching the three sluggish divisions?

By year end, sales increase to $660 million and profits reach $2 million, as shown below:

Selected Financial and Productivity Information
(Revenues and Profits in $ Millions)

	Third Year	*Second Year*
Revenues	$660	$602
Profits	$2	($2)
Employees	1,838	1,709
Revenues per Employee (Actual $)	$359,086	$352,253
Profits per Employee (Actual $)	$1,088	($1,170)

At this critical juncture in your tenure as CEO, Bill Faragut tells you he is not pleased with your performance. He requests another companywide productivity assessment.

To discover how FaraCom rates in this productivity assessment, turn to Chapter 24, page 101.

CHAPTER 19

Exploiting the Psychological Type of Each Division President

Given a greater appreciation among your division presidents of their unique personalities and styles, you decide to take psychological typing one step further by putting each of your division presidents' direct reports through the full Myers-Briggs Type Indicator assessment. To accomplish this, you hire Eric Marchant, one of the country's best psychological type specialists and part of the earlier effort, to administer the Myers-Briggs Type Indicator to the more than 70 executives. You also conduct a 360-degree review with peers, subordinates, and superiors of the seven division presidents to determine how their associates view them. The 360-degree review involves getting feedback from the full circle of associates surrounding an executive through written and verbal assessments. It allows the executive to find out exactly how he or she is perceived by work associates.

The whole project takes six months to complete, but at the end, your seven division presidents claim that they understand themselves and their key managers better than ever before. New ideas and approaches for improving productivity based on psychological type proliferate. First, your seven division presidents get much better at quickly identifying natural talent in an area and exploiting it for the benefit of the company and the individual. Janice Kofoed, the new president of cable television operations, describes her experience, "With the help of an MBTI assessment, I can discern a manager's aptitude for and interest in a particular assignment. It's a much more productive way to assign responsibilities." Second, every division management team develops stronger bonds of understanding, appreciation, and trust. Alan Peay, the new president of book publishing, expresses his own feelings, "I never thought I would experience this, but the level of commitment and unity among my new team has never been greater. We draw upon each other's strengths to mitigate against each others' weaknesses. It's almost miraculous how it works when we're solving problems and planning for the future."

Slowly, but purposefully, you begin customizing the development of each of your seven division presidents, treating no two presidents or divisions the same. You realize that each division management team represents a unique mix of temperaments, perspectives, and capabilities. As you tailor your efforts to each divisional management team, you take particular pride in the progress of the four division presidents who switched assignments. Janice Kofoed formulates a comprehensive long-term strategy for cable television operations, something Sean Cope could never have achieved. Likewise, Sean Cope fine-tunes and adapts the business system established by Kofoed for catalog sales and direct marketing to perform at levels beyond Kofoed's grasp. The shift between Harshaw and Peay also bears fruit, allowing Peay to completely reorganize the book publishing division and Harshaw to unify the magazine publishing culture around a clear common purpose. In each case, the new division presidents brought the necessary talents and perspectives to bear on their new situations. In a sense, you think to yourself, building a business is like building a house: first, you plan it, then you lay the foundation, then you frame it, wire and plumb it, roof it, dry-wall it, brick it, paint it, finish it, furnish it, and finally you live in it and maintain it. Each stage of building requires different skills and capabilities until the house is completed, and then it must be maintained.

By year's end, sales climb to $850 million and profits grow to $50 million:

Selected Financial and Productivity Information
(Revenues and Profits in $ Millions)

	First Year	Previous Year
Revenues	$861	$748
Profits	$50	$10
Employees	1,911	1,865
Revenues per Employee (Actual $)	$450,549	$401,072
Profits per Employee (Actual $)	$26,164	$5,362

At the first of the year, Bill Faragut insists on another companywide productivity assessment to identify just how much improvement your efforts have actually accomplished over the last year, and you readily agree.

To find out how FaraCom stacks up in this next productivity assessment, turn to Chapter 24, page 101.

CHAPTER 20

Perfecting the Three Fields of Work Among Your Division Presidents

The insights gained from exploring the three generic fields of work in the MetaWork System have greatly enhanced your ability to work with your seven division presidents on improving their own and their people's productivity. Alan Peay, president of magazine publishing, admits to focusing only on efficiency and effectiveness while neglecting talent development, relationship building, knowledge searching, and value creation. He says, "I now spend more time thinking about the other fields of work (developing talent and relationships and discovering knowledge and value) than I ever did before. It has helped me expand my own capabilities as well as take advantage of the strengths of others."

You continue using the complete idea of three generic fields of work to help your division presidents better understand the differences between each of the fields and how to monitor performance in each more precisely. Through a series of discussions with your seven division presidents, you develop your own terminology for the three generic fields of work: completing work, unifying work, and magnifying work. Completing work means figuring out what work needs to be done and how; its focus centers on efficiency, effectiveness, power, and results. Unifying work refers to the drawing together of skills and people in a common purpose; it focuses on talents, relationships, networking, and unity. Magnifying work signifies the expansion and elevation of work efforts; its focus revolves around knowledge, worth, value, and breakthroughs. After developing your own definitions for

87

the three generic fields of work, you begin discussing conceptual scenarios about their application. With respect to completing work, you and your seven division presidents agree that everything in this field focuses on efficiently and effectively getting results, which, though vital, can push people and organizations into a highly reactive mode, unless they combine it with unifying and magnifying work. In the field of unifying work, you agree that focusing on developing skills and building relationships helps people and organizations perform more meaningful work and foster greater unity. In magnifying the work field, you agree that knowledge and application are the keys, citing examples of people such as Bill Gates, who broaden and apply their knowledge to create more value for more people.

Remaining in a probing discussion mode during management meetings and off-site retreats for the next several months, you work with your seven division presidents as a group and one-on-one, wrestling with questions such as, "How can FaraCom divisions do things more effectively and more efficiently?" "How can we develop greater talents and better relationships?" "How can our people discover greater knowledge in order to create more value for our customers and other stakeholders?"

To your delight, your division presidents begin conducting similar probing discussions with their management teams. Lisa Harshaw, president of book publishing, sums up the feelings of your division presidents, "We have learned how to think about and improve productivity in three very different fields of work, and it's making a big difference in our operations."

By the end of your third year as CEO, you see the fruits of this transfer of learning as sales reach $840 million and profits climb past $60 million:

Selected Financial and Productivity Information
(Revenues and Profits in $ Millions)

	First Year	*Previous Year*
Revenues	$841	$725
Profits	$61	$30
Employees	1,829	1,817
Revenues per Employee (Actual $)	$459,814	$399,009
Profits per Employee (Actual $)	$33,352	$16,511

It does not surprise you when Bill Faragut requests another company-wide productivity assessment at this crucial point, but you quickly embrace the idea as a good way to measure last year's improvement and reinforce the need for further improvements.

To find out how FaraCom fares in this next round of assessments, turn to Chapter 24, page 101.

CHAPTER 21

Customizing the Franklin Time-Management Program

As you enter your third year as CEO, you accept the fact that the productivity improvements achieved by FaraCom employees with the Franklin Day Planner program may have reached their limit. In order to squeeze out more productivity, you decide to customize the Franklin program to your company's own needs, adding priorities developed by each of the divisions to aid people in their daily planning.

Working with Franklin Quest personnel and your own staff of trainers, over a three-month period you assist each of the divisions in developing a customized approach to daily planning that utilizes a priority system tailored to each division's operations. For example, Stephen Ferreira, president of film and video production, identifies four overriding priorities that division employees use in daily planning: master scheduling, production budgeting, talent development, and cash-flow balancing. Employees in Ferreira's division are asked to carefully consider these four priorities in their daily planning and evaluation activities.

As other divisions follow a similar course of outlining common divisional priorities, a new set of divisional pages for the day planners are introduced during a second companywide seminar on "Enhancing the Day Planner." The new pages facilitate more focused employee planning, coordination, and review by listing divisional priorities and providing space for prioritizing daily tasks on the basis of overall division priorities.

By the end of your third year as CEO, every employee has gone through the second phase of training, learning how to use the new customized pages and planning system to further enhance productivity companywide. However, sales increase to only $720 million by the end of the year, with profits increasing modestly to $6 million, as shown below:

Selected Financial and Productivity Information
(Revenues and Profits in $ Millions)

	First Year	Previous Year
Revenues	$719	$669
Profits	$6	$4
Employees	1,938	1,827
Revenues per Employee (Actual $)	$371,001	$366,174
Profits per Employee (Actual $)	$3,096	$2,189

When Bill Faragut asks for another companywide productivity assessment, you feel somewhat concerned that you have reached the end of improvements with the day-planning system, but you hope that the new customized pages and application of FaraCom priorities will further enhance productivity next year.

To find out the results of this next round of productivity assessments, turn to Chapter 24, page 101.

CHAPTER 22

Stressing True North Principles

As you embark on your third year as CEO, you conclude that the most significant productivity improvements across the seven divisions will come from further application of Covey's "true north" principles. The simple idea that everyone in an organization can act on principle instead of procedure or specified behavior offers remarkable power in terms of unifying, coordinating, and motivating employees.

You stress the fundamental principles driving FaraCom as a whole, plus the development of secondary principles for each division to help employees make better decisions and take more profitable daily action. In the catalog sales and direct marketing division, for instance, Janice Kofoed establishes three fundamental principles after several weeks of discussion and analysis with her management team: (1) Never offend a customer, (2) always cross sell (sell other products in the catalog), and (3) diligently seek customer feedback. In her own words she describes the impact of these principles, "I am actually amazed at how thirsty our people were for such simplicity and clarity. Now, they feel more confident making their own decisions, which has boosted morale, increased sales, and improved productivity."

You're thrilled to see people throughout the company actually plan their days based on principles, pay attention to their different roles, and consistently eliminate unnecessary work processes and procedures, cutting out the misuse of resources, wasted time, and most office politics. "First things first," at FaraCom comes to mean principles over procedures and empowerment over control. In each division, employees can easily explain the division's vision and objectives, not only in broad terms, but also in terms of their own jobs and daily routines.

A few months later in a meeting with your seven division presidents, you ask them to summarize the effects of the Covey planning system. Sean Cope, president of cable television operations, says, "I didn't think I would ever get out of my dependence upon procedures, schedules, and task plans to get results, but this new focus on principles has given me a greater appreciation for the latitude that diverse people need in order to work together and to bring their unique strengths to bear for the good of the whole." Mona Sork, president of retail operations, puts it this way: "My first reaction was this stuff is way too soft. It just didn't seem to have the power to make things happen in an organization—but I was wrong. I now realize that clearly identifying principles that govern general and specific situations provides the deepest and most comprehensive organizational continuity." Alan Peay, president of magazine publishing, responds, "Decision making has always come easily to me, but I have relied on a very structured, disciplined approach in the past, which doesn't always work when you're in a crisis or entering new ground. This approach has caused me to think more deeply about what I do every day, to ask questions I've never considered. It really has improved my productivity as president of the division and expanded my horizons." David Zollweg, president of software and CD-ROM publishing, comments, "I've always known that principles, if understood, could marshall resources and people better than anything else in a situation, but I never believed an organization could consistently operate that way until now." Janice Kofoed, president of catalog sales and direct marketing, adds, "When we help our people understand the appropriate principles involved, they can manage themselves. It's beautiful." Stephen Ferreira, president of film and video production, exclaims, "My people have doubled their productivity because they know what's important and can act and think for themselves." Lisa Harshaw, president of book publishing, sums it up nicely: "In an organization, people are always putting different priorities on tasks and responsibilities, and everybody puts something different first. But now we have a philosophy and an approach that allow us to put the same things first. The people in my division have grown as a result."

You're pleased with the feedback and the results of the Covey planning system and its focus on principles. It has truly transformed the

FaraCom organization. At the end of your third year as CEO, sales reach $835 million and profits grow to $62 million:

Selected Financial and Productivity Information
(Revenues and Profits in $ Millions)

	Third Year	*Second Year*
Revenues	$835	$710
Profits	$62	$26
Employees	1,878	1,812
Revenues per Employee (Actual $)	$444,622	$391,832
Profits per Employee (Actual $)	$33,014	$14,349

After the year ends, you feel supremely confident when Bill Faragut asks for another companywide productivity assessment, because you know the results will prove the wisdom of your decisions over the past three years.

To find out how FaraCom fares in this next round of productivity assessments, turn to Chapter 24, page 101.

CHAPTER 23

Navigating EmpowerTech's Productivity Network

Early in your third year as CEO of FaraCom, you begin to see EmpowerTech's enormous potential for improving productivity, though you conclude that the true payoff can come only when people become fully immersed in the system. While the initial results have proven attractive, increasing productivity measurably, you perceive that the organization has reached a plateau that will require extensive training to tap the potential of the system. After a senior management meeting, Lisa Harshaw, president of book publishing, asks to talk with you. She begins, "I believe the EmpowerTech system can move us toward unparalleled productivity in the future, but we're stalled. Sure, all the divisions are operating pretty well right now, but we've only captured the tip of the iceberg in terms of productivity gains. I think we need another big push to capture more of the potential benefits of this system." After a few minutes of further discussion, you thank Harshaw for her input and then spend the rest of the week pondering FaraCom's situation.

Deciding to incur even more expense, you bring in a group of EmpowerTech consultants to design a high-tech training program that will take FaraCom to that next plateau. Their recommendation seems simple—the more FaraCom employees learn how to maneuver on the FaraCom network (FaraNet), the more they will find new uses, applications, and ways to coordinate their efforts with others. The investment in training will cost another $5 million over the next year, bringing the total price tag for implementation to $20 million.

As you struggle with whether or not to move forward, you allow several weeks to pass, unconsciously hoping the organization will somehow move forward on its own. Eventually, however, you realize the company will rest on the present plateau until you infuse a fresh round of training and education for all FaraCom employees. In a series of meetings with your seven division presidents and their management teams, you further confirm your suspicion that the company has obtained about all the benefits of E-mail, project scheduling, and information sharing it can get and that other applications, such as on-line strategic planning, front-end-loaded document preparation that maximizes input on the front-end rather than on the back-end, customer loyalty tracking with daily updates on feedback, continuous employee surveying, and a host of other possibilities, cannot come into play until people become much more comfortable navigating the FaraNet. It also becomes obvious to you that the expanse of information outside the organization through services such as America On-Line and CompuServe and new software for navigating the global Internet can also provide a wealth of benefits for FaraCom, if only they can tap them on a regular basis, as part of their daily jobs.

Before the end of the year, you decide to move forward with the training and the $5 million more in expenses. At year end, sales reach $770 million with profits climbing to $30 million, indicating the growing operational strength of each division. As you think about FaraCom's financial and productivity results (shown in the table below), you realize how far the company has come in three short years.

Selected Financial and Productivity Information
(Revenues and Profits in $ Millions)

	Third Year	*Second Year*
Revenues	$769	$681
Profits	$31	$8
Employees	1,958	1,845
Revenues per Employee (Actual $)	$392,748	$369,106
Profits per Employee (Actual $)	$15,832	$4,336

You remain confident that the future will unfold productively, but when Bill Faragut asks for another companywide productivity assessment, you wonder whether he's losing confidence in your initiatives with EmpowerTech. You wonder whether you should pay more attention to specific divisional operating issues and concerns. Reluctantly, you accept his request, hoping it will at least prove constructive.

To find out how FaraCom scores in this productivity assessment, turn to Chapter 24, page 101

CHAPTER 24

Examining FaraCom's Second Productivity Review

Bill Faragut again picks Ernst & Young to perform the companywide productivity assessment because Ernst & Young's long experience with FaraCom will bring continuity to the process. As they did a year ago, Ernst & Young once again bases its investigation on three major measurements: value added per employee, productivity comparison to "best-in-world" competitors, and FaraCom's productivity improvements over the past year. As you saw in Chapter 14, the value-added measure subtracts the total dollar cost of all materials purchased from the total dollar revenues of products and services sold to obtain a total dollar value-added figure, divided by the total number of FaraCom employees, resulting in a value-added-per-employee measurement. Three years ago the value-added figure per employee hovered around $100,000.

The "best-in-world" productivity comparison measure averages the published sales per employee, profits per employee, and other available data from ten highly successful communications and entertainment companies with operations similar in whole or part to FaraCom's. The combined data results in a "best-in-world" comparison index of 1,000, to which FaraCom can be compared.

The internal FaraCom Productivity Index measures improvement in a variety of areas, such as quality, errors, output, rework, and resources utilized. A composite number of "100" represents the baseline (the point just before you assumed your current job).

At this point in *The Productivity Game*, you can switch to a different decision-making track, based on what you learn from this second productivity review. Before you consider doing so, however, spend some time

101

studying the following assessments and table summarizing the performance and productivity outcomes of the nine different tracks that have led up to this chapter:

> Chapter 15, Refining a Companywide Strategy and Theme—If you pursued this course of deploying your own unique talents to build productivity, you increased productivity respectably.

> Chapter 16, Continuing to Develop Strong Divisional Strategies and Cultures—If you chose to deploy your own unique capabilities by helping each division fine tune strategies and cultures, you increased productivity even further.

> Chapter 17, Increasing Emphasis on Strategic Thinking—If you deployed yourself by strengthening strategic thinking in your subordinates, you caused productivity to drop substantially.

> Chapter 18, Further Encouraging the Seven Division Presidents to Pursue Their Own Productivity Agendas—If you chose to build the productivity of your seven presidents by encouraging their own agendas, you caused a serious productivity decline.

> Chapter 19, Exploiting the Psychological Type of Each Division President - If you focused on increasing the productivity of your seven presidents through psychological typing and deployment, you accomplished a stunning improvement in productivity.

> Chapter 20, Perfecting the Three Dimensions of Work Among Your Division Presidents—If you worked on the productivity of your seven presidents by stressing the three fields of work, you raised productivity to new heights.

> Chapter 21, Customizing the Franklin Time Management Program—If you picked this course for improving companywide productivity, you brought about an unfortunate decline in productivity.

> Chapter 22, Stressing True North Principles—If you focused on companywide productivity by relying on Covey's methodologies, you increased productivity nicely.

> Chapter 23, Navigating EmpowerTech's Productivity Network—If you pushed the EmpowerTech system to build productivity companywide, you accomplished a respectable increase in productivity.

Chapter	Revenues	Profits	Employees	Revenues/ Employee	Profits per Employee	Value- Added Index	"Best-in- World" Index	Fara- Com Index	Composite Ranking
15	$760	$31	1,876	$405,117	$16,524	134,000	763	129	6
16	$802	$29	1,909	$420,115	$15,191	128,000	842	137	5
17	$648	$.2	1,963	$330,107	$102	95,000	521	98	9
18	$660	$2	1,838	$359,086	$1,088	107,000	599	101	8
19	$861	$50	1,911	$450,549	$26,164	154,000	855	161	3
20	$841	$61	1,829	$459,814	$33,352	158,000	888	164	1
21	$719	$6	1,938	$371,001	$3,096	111,000	691	106	7
22	$835	$62	1,878	$444,622	$33,014	155,000	836	162	2
23	$769	$31	1,958	$392,748	$15,832	132,000	840	138	4
Benchmark						100,000	1,000	100	—

With this comprehensive overview in mind, you can now choose to explore one of the tracks you did not select earlier, or you can move forward with one of the nine following options.

If you choose to maintain your focus on maximizing your own productivity by building an integrated strategy and theme for the company, turn to Chapter 25, Reaping the Fruits of FaraCom's Integrated Strategy, page 105.

If you decide to continue concentrating on your own productivity by helping the divisions develop strong strategies and cultures, turn to Chapter 26, Spinning Out FaraCom's Divisions, page 109.

If you still believe that individual productivity and the development of your seven division presidents' strategic management capabilities represents the best course of action, turn to Chapter 27, Continuing the Emphasis on Strategic Management Training, page 113.

If you still believe that your seven division presidents should set their own productivity improvement agendas, turn to Chapter 28, Continuing to Set Divisional Productivity Agendas, page 117.

If you desire to continue focusing on the psychological type of division executives as the key to productivity improvement, turn to Chapter 29, Gaining Deeper Understanding of Psychological Type, page 121.

If you want to further explore and exploit the three dimensions of work, turn to Chapter 30, Taking the Three Fields of Work to the Next Level, page 125.

If you want to continue enhancing Franklin's time-management program companywide, turn to Chapter 31, Holding Firm to Time Management, page 129.

If you still believe the Covey Leadership approach represents the best path, turn to Chapter 32, Taking First Things First, a Second Step, page 133.

If you believe EmpowerTech's technology-driven system provides the key to greater companywide productivity, turn to Chapter 33, Cruising the FaraNet, page 137.

CHAPTER 25

Reaping the Fruits of FaraCom's Integrated Strategy

Your fourth year as CEO of FaraCom brings a wave of pleasant surprises when the public's appetite for values-based entertainment explodes throughout the United States. Few companies in the communications and entertainment industry seem as well positioned as FaraCom to capitalize on the accelerating demand for values-based movies, videos, CDs, software, books, and magazines. Thanks to your efforts to integrate the company's divisions behind this vision, FaraCom receives enormous media attention.

In September, a front page article in *The New York Times*'s business section touts FaraCom as "the most values-oriented and productivity-conscious company of the late 1990s." The article quotes you and Bill Faragut extensively, which generates a flurry of follow-up articles in other periodicals, such as *Fortune, BusinessWeek, Forbes, Training, HR Magazine,* and *Training & Development,* all of them praising your efforts to maximize your own productivity by concentrating on the company's integrated values-based strategy. Within a matter of weeks, you receive eight calls from executive recruiting firms trying to interest you in leaving FaraCom for what they each describe as a "greater" opportunity. Though you feel content in your present job, one of the opportunities does interest you: the CEOship of the strategically afloat Viacom-Paramount conglomerate. After a series of confidential discussions with members of the Viacom-Paramount board of directors, you seriously consider leaving FaraCom. The chairman of the

Board, Ted Thornock, offers you a salary, bonus, and stock-option package worth several million dollars a year.

When Bill Faragut finds out about the offer, he storms into your office and for the next three days spends most of his time pleading with you to stay. His arguments do little to persuade you because the opportunity at Viacom-Paramount would allow you to expand your influence in the industry and either Janice Kofoed or Stephen Ferreira could easily replace you at FaraCom. To your amazement, Faragut offers to take the company public and give you 20 percent of the stock. Such an arrangement would probably increase your net worth by $50 to $75 million in the next year. The offer dumbfounds you. You didn't think Faragut would ever give up that much of his precious stock. Of course, you agree to think seriously about the offer.

That evening, your old friend Jack Eisenhower, the managing partner of Ernst & Young, calls you at home. After the usual niceties, he asks if you'd consider coming back to E&Y as the managing partner overseeing worldwide consulting. Once again, the offer astounds you. You discuss the possibility with Jack for the next hour and a half. He tells you that he'd like you to apply your strategy integration skills to redesign the firm's consulting practice throughout the world, saying, "You are the management committee's first choice. You'll have *carte blanche* to do whatever you want to build a world-class consulting operation." You promise you'll get back to him on Monday.

Instead of going into the office on Thursday, you leave for your favorite place on earth, your seaside home at Boothbay Harbor on the Maine coast, to contemplate your options. You spend Thursday and Friday reviewing these three incredible opportunities, and you eventually conclude that your decision to maximize your own productivity started it all. By placing your own productivity at the center of your decision making, you not only performed consistently at your own peak, you set a strong example for your division presidents and the rest of the company. In retrospect, it seems paradoxical that a decision to focus on yourself could produce so many benefits for others—division presidents, company employees, FaraCom customers, industry competitors, and the public.

Saturday morning you arise before 6:00 A.M. to watch the sunrise from your deck and summarize everything you've been thinking about for two days. Using a simple 3″ × 3″ grid, you rate each of your options from 1 to 3 (1 representing your first choice) in terms of maximizing productivity, wealth, and influence, as follows:

	Maximizing Productivity	Maximizing Wealth	Maximizing Influence
Remain at FaraCom and become a 20% shareholder	3	1	3
Join Viacom-Paramount as CEO	2	2	1
Return to Ernst & Young as managing partner over Consulting	1	3	2

After returning from your long weekend in Maine, you tell Faragut, Thornock, and Eisenhower that you'll give them your decision after the first of the year, a short three weeks hence. In the meantime, year-end results push FaraCom over $1 billion in sales and $100 million in profits, as shown below:

Selected Financial and Productivity Information
(Revenues and Profits in $ Millions)

	Fourth Year	Third Year
Revenues	$1,003	$760
Profits	101	31
Employees	2,008	1,876
Revenues per Employee (Actual $)	$499,501	$405,117
Profits per Employee (Actual $)	$50,299	$1,164

The year-end results spur another round of media attention, which pleases Bill Faragut enormously. You, however, attempt to remain somewhat detached and objective because you still face a life-shaping decision. What will you do? Down one path lies a tremendous opportunity to maximize productivity; down another lies the promise of unsurpassed wealth; while down yet another lies a chance to influence an entire industry. Which possibility attracts you the most? As you wrestle with these and similar questions, Ted

Thornock calls to tell you that he must know your decision by tomorrow. Time's up. What will you do?

If you decide to stay at FaraCom, turn to Chapter 34, page 141.

If you want to move to Viacom-Paramount, turn to Chapter 35, page 145.

If you choose to return to Ernst & Young, turn to Chapter 36, page 147.

CHAPTER 26

Spinning Out FaraCom's Divisions

Stimulated by the success of FaraCom's first two spin-outs (Cable TV and Software/CD-ROM), you spend the next several months spinning out the other five divisions. Under this strategy, FaraCom becomes a holding company for seven vibrant communications and entertainment companies and establishes a new model for the industry. This startling turn of events attracts tremendous media attention, as reporters scurry to find out what's happening at FaraCom, and their glowing articles bring a number of acquisition and alliance opportunities to your doorstep. Having already decided to focus the bulk of your own attention on external acquisitions that can fit under the FaraCom umbrella, you complete six acquisitions by the end of the year: Media Play, a communications and entertainment chain of superstores; Family Favorites, a new values-based video rental operation; Interactive Films International, a CD-based motion picture production company that produces interactive movies; *Internet*, a magazine devoted to "cruising the Internet"; Prentice Hall Books, an employee buy-out from Viacom-Paramount; and Magavision, a new cable television magazine network.

You acquire each of these companies with the same formula you used to spin out the divisions of FaraCom: 33 percent to FaraCom, 33 percent to management, 33 percent to the public. Your three basic tenets of innovative leadership, market dominance, and radical improvement take on greater importance as FaraCom grows rapidly, and that accelerated growth, in turn, serves to entrench and strengthen the three fundamental principles.

At the end of your fourth year as CEO, sales reach $1.1 billion, as shown below:

Selected Financial and Productivity Information
(Revenues and Profits in $ Millions)

	Fourth Year	*Third Year*
Revenues	$1,104	$802
Profits	63	29
Employees	2,276	1,909
Revenues per Employee (Actual $)	$485,062	$420,115
Profits per Employee (Actual $)	$27,680	$15,191

At the beginning of your fifth year as CEO of FaraCom, some of the operations indicate a growing need for your personal help in implementing strategy and strengthening culture. You wonder whether you should spend more time with the individual companies under the FaraCom umbrella or whether you should keep your mind on external acquisitions. While you're considering these two possibilities, a third option arises out of the blue: an opportunity to acquire NBC from General Electric. Evidently, people at General Electric have been watching your work at FaraCom with great interest and have decided to approach you about buying 60 percent of NBC. According to GE's plan, the remaining 40 percent would eventually go public. The GE representative makes the feelings of the board of directors at General Electric quite clear: "We need a new kind of CEO in the communications and entertainment industry to manage NBC, and, while we've been looking for the last year, we have found no one else who meets our expectations." They have been studying you quite closely over the last several months and have concluded that you may be the perfect person to take over an operation like NBC.

While you agree to discussions with executives and board members at General Electric, you worry that the NBC acquisition would dwarf the rest of FaraCom's budding operations and consume all of your time and attention. However, the NBC deal may represent the best way to maximize your own productivity, allowing you to apply your talents and capabilities to a really breathtaking challenge. Wouldn't it be wonderful to revitalize a huge but struggling TV network?

You carefully consider the three options: continuing external acquisitions, directing your energies internally to build strategies and cultures in the acquired and spun-out companies, or acquiring NBC and repositioning it on the information superhighway. The following $3'' \times 3''$ grid summarizes your rating of each of the three options in terms of productivity, growth, and strategic impact (a 1 indicates your first choice in each cell):

	Maximizing Productivity	Maximizing Growth	Maximizing Strategic Impact
Focus on external acquisitions	3	1	2
Direct energies internally to build strategies and cultures	1	3	3
Acquire NBC	2	2	1

What will you do? Do you feel more motivated to maximize productivity, achieve spectacular growth, or make a lasting strategic impact on an entire industry?

After pondering your rankings and envisioning yourself in each of these three scenarios, you finally select the one that attracts you the most.

If you choose to focus on external acquisitions, turn to Chapter 37, page 149.

If you decide to direct your energies internally to build strong strategies and cultures in each of the spin-outs and acquired companies, turn to Chapter 38, page 151.

If you want to move forward with the NBC acquisition, turn to Chapter 39, page 153.

CHAPTER 27

Continuing the Emphasis on Strategic Management Training

As you begin your fourth year as FaraCom's CEO, you feel extreme pressure to increase productivity companywide, yet you shy away from shifting your focus from training management teams in each division to resolve issues of strategic management: strategic thinking, culture building, change management, continuous improvement, and high performance.

Having already taken the senior divisional management teams and the next level of functional management in each division through extensive training, you now find yourself waiting and hoping for the productivity payoff. In all your communications with division presidents, you reinforce the importance of strategic management skills. You also attempt to embrace the learning organization philosophy, encouraging everyone in each of the divisions to continue growing and developing personally, as well as managerially.

As the first few months of your fourth year as CEO pass by, you realize that the necessary improvements in productivity and growth and profitability have not materialized, a fact that prompts you to question your own productivity and to wonder whether you have been traveling the wrong road over the last few years. You decide to ask Sean Cope, president of cable television operations and always a good barometer on current conditions, to give you some candid feedback. Somewhat surprised at your request, he responds, "Do you want the truth?"

"Of course!"

113

"Sometimes people ask for candid feedback, but aren't really prepared to receive it."

"I'm ready," you say with some frustration and anxiety about what he will say.

"I think we're spending too much time on a lot of conceptual crap."

Shocked by his candor, you counter, "Why didn't you express this earlier?"

"I tried. You didn't want to listen."

Stunned by the interchange, you spend the next few days pondering your situation.

To make matters worse, Bill Faragut makes it clear to you that if you don't turn things around quickly and improve results by the end of the year, he'll replace you as CEO. While this possibility distresses you and heightens your concern about whether you've made the right choices during the past few years, you still believe, albeit less confidently, that your focus on strategic management will pay off eventually. On the other hand, you know that Bill Faragut will not allow you the necessary time for that to happen.

Over the next few days, you come up with three alternative courses of action. First, you might pursue a major downsizing project to reduce costs, improve profitability, and increase productivity. Second, you might initiate an employee buy-out of FaraCom to remove Bill Faragut from the picture. Third, you might take FaraCom's 75 top executives, the management teams from each of the divisions, to a week-long retreat where you can impress upon them the necessity of achieving major, dramatic improvements before the end of the year. You rate these three options on a scale of 1 to 3, (1 representing the best choice) in terms of maximizing productivity, maximizing change, and maximizing profits. The grid below summarizes your rankings:

	Maximizing Productivity	Maximizing Change	Maximizing Profits
Major downsizing project	1	2	3
An employee buy-out	3	1	2
A week-long retreat	2	3	1

It all depends on what motivates you the most: maximum productivity, sweeping change, or impressive profits.

Now, four months into your fourth year as CEO, you must decide which course will most likely get things back on track and restore Bill Faragut's confidence in you.

If you choose to pursue a major downsizing project, turn to Chapter 40, page 155.

If you decide to initiate an employee buy-out to remove Bill Faragut from the chairmanship and ownership of FaraCom, turn to Chapter 41, page 157.

If you want to get FaraCom's top 75 executives together for a week-long, intense discussion on how to bring about dramatic improvements, turn to Chapter 42, page 159.

CHAPTER 28

Continuing to Set Divisional Productivity Agendas

Satisfied with the progress of Stephen Ferreira and Lisa Harshaw in terms of productivity improvements, you continue to work with Sean Cope, Mona Sork, and Alan Peay by holding additional retreats to discuss innovative approaches. Watchfully, you let Janice Kofoed and David Zollweg remain intent on managing growth, assuming that their efforts will naturally result in productivity increases in their two operations—catalog sales/direct marketing and software/CD-ROM publishing.

Continued progress with Sean Cope, Mona Sork, and Alan Peay will, you hope, achieve necessary productivity improvements for the coming year. During your retreats with these three division presidents, you take heart from one simple reality: Different executives approach productivity differently. This reality allows you to take a more aggressive position with the three division presidents who are struggling with productivity agendas. They want it and need it. Since Harshaw and Ferreira, along with Kofoed and Zollweg, do not need the same kind of direction from you, you can concentrate your time and effort on the three division presidents who do most need your help. Although you feel disappointed that it's taken you so long to figure this out, you now realize that if you dive in with both feet, working hard to help the three division presidents build productivity in their operations, you just might get the results you want.

The series of retreats leads to the development of a common theme: the concept of productivity constraints. A productivity constraint amounts to a bottleneck anywhere in the operation, be it with an individual, a team, a system, a process, anything, in other words, that gets in the way of greater

117

results or increased productivity. This single idea becomes the organizing principle for Cope, Sork, and Peay, and it helps each identify and resolve one bottleneck after another in their operations. For example, Mona Sork, president of retail operations, and her management team quickly identified and eliminated three major productivity constraints in the merchandising area: an antiquated delivery receiving process, which they updated and streamlined; too many people involved in making merchandise display decisions, which they reduced; and lots of red tape and unnecessary approvals in the product-returns procedure, which they eliminated.

Similar progress in all three divisions thrills you, and you hope it will send a clear message to Bill Faragut and the board of directors about FaraCom's future prospects. You also feel grateful to Elyahu M. Goldratt, author of *The Goal*, and *It's Not Luck*, whose compelling books on continuous productivity improvements guided you and your three division presidents to identify the productivity constraints within their divisions.

Mona Sork sums up the feelings of the three division presidents best, saying, "When you first asked us to set our own productivity agendas, I didn't know where to start. We tried a number of things that didn't seem to have much impact. I found myself yearning for more guidance from someone. When Alan Peay brought our attention to *The Goal*, and *It's Not Luck*, by Goldratt, it laid the groundwork for using this idea of productivity constraints to make a huge difference in the way we manage our operations. Now we look for bottlenecks anywhere and everywhere, and then we get rid of them, one by one. It's a wonderful way to manage."

At the end of your fourth year as CEO of FaraCom, you enjoy a strong increase in revenues and profits to $750 million and $20 million, respectively, as shown below:

Selected Financial and Productivity Information
(Revenues and Profits in $ Millions)

	Fourth Year	*Third Year*
Revenues	$749	$660
Profits	20	2
Employees	1,980	1,838
Revenues per Employee (Actual $)	$378,283	$359,086
Profits per Employee (Actual $)	$10,101	$1,088

While these numbers diminish some of the pressure from Bill Faragut and the board regarding productivity improvements, you know that they're still not happy with the overall results of your leadership. When you come out and ask Faragut point blank to tell you how he really feels, he confesses that he's disappointed in your leadership and honestly thinks FaraCom should have progressed much further by this point in time. His words cause you several sleepless nights and ignite a lot of rethinking about alternative courses of action for the future. You simply must demonstrate impressive progress within the year.

After a few weeks, three alternatives emerge as your most viable options: continue on the same course, hoping that it will bear greater fruit next year; apply the idea of productivity constraints and removing bottlenecks to all FaraCom operations as quickly as possible; or turn your gaze outward, seeking acquisitions that could infuse new growth and profitability into the company. To analyze how the three options will fuel productivity, continuous improvement, and change, you create a $3'' \times 3''$ grid, ranking from 1 to 3 each of the options (1 represents your best option):

	Maximizing Change	Maximizing Continuous Improvement	Maximizing Productivity
Continuing the current course	3	2	1
Applying the idea of productivity constraints companywide	2	1	2
Turning attention outside toward acquisitions	1	3	3

While this summary of your options paints a clear picture of your future prospects, it can't make this tough and difficult decision for you. Which motivates you the most: creating dramatic change, maximizing continuous improvement, or pushing productivity to the limit? You must decide before the end of the week.

If you decide to continue your current course, turn to Chapter 43, page 163.

If you wish to apply the idea of productivity constraints companywide, turn to Chapter 44, page 165.

If you choose to pursue external acquisitions, turn to Chapter 45, page 169.

CHAPTER 29

Gaining Deeper Understanding of Psychological Type

As the top 73 FaraCom executives gain a deeper awareness of natural preferences and psychological type, they find it much easier to assign people to the right work. Shifting of assignments occurs frequently as they match natural preferences and psychological type to market conditions and company situations, and a new culture begins emerging at FaraCom. Although you must still take care that people do not abuse the system, namely, letting themselves get pigeon-holed, devalued, or overvalued, the overall impact proves exhilarating and empowering.

You begin to recognize the pattern of shifting that works best among your managers: a two-step development cycle in which a visionary, conceptual, and future-thinking executive lays the groundwork in a function or business unit and then moves on to allow an objective, analytical, organized, and tough-minded executive to execute the vision.

For example, as your fourth year as CEO of FaraCom unfolds, Kofoed's shift from catalog sales to cable television operations proves brilliant when she defines a whole new operating approach for cable television that greatly multiplies the outside sources of programming and increases opportunities for syndications to other cable networks. Likewise, the move of Sean Cope from cable television operations to catalog sales and direct marketing pays off because Kofoed's clear strategic focus on list management and telephone competence allows him to adapt at a moment's notice to changes in the marketplace, integrating new lists and adjusting telephone pitches with ease. This same kind of harmonious relationship occurs between Harshaw and Peay, who also switched their assignments— Harshaw from books to magazines, and Peay from magazines to books. Harshaw's exceptional ability at forging common purpose and building unity continues to breathe new life and empowerment into the well-organized and disciplined magazine publishing division. Similarly, Peay's strong orientation toward organizational effectiveness and operational efficiency keeps adding new discipline and structure to the unified and committed book-publishing division.

By year end, sales reach $1 billion and profits climb to over $100 million, as shown below:

Selected Financial and Productivity Information
(Revenues and Profits in $ Millions)

	Fourth Year	*Third Year*
Revenues	$1,038	$861
Profits	104	50
Employees	2,064	1,911
Revenues per Employee (Actual $)	$502,907	$450,549
Profits per Employee (Actual $)	$50,388	$26,164

Soon after the first of the year, you discover, with the help of your seven division presidents, that the development cycle should include yet a third step, which falls between the two previous steps. While this culturalizing or institutionalizing step is not as clear-cut as the other two, nonetheless, when carefully planned and executed, it helps remove obstacles and bottlenecks in implementation and execution of specific strategies.

The new three-step cycle works this way: A visionary, conceptual, future-thinking executive sets the direction and then turns over the reins to a culture-building, people-sensitive, and principle-centered executive, who establishes the cultural norms and who then passes the baton to an organized, structurally oriented, analytical, objective, and adaptive executive who concentrates on implementation and execution within the parameters set by the visionary direction and the cultural norms. In your own mind, you think of these three steps as knowing, being, and doing. "Knowing executives" probe into the inner workings of the marketplace to understand its economic logic, the needs of customers, and the capabilities of the company to shape the future. "Being executives" pay close attention to matching people with assignments, articulating operating philosophies and principles, and generally establishing the norms of the organizational culture, which, in turn, establishes the perfect environment for execution and implementation. With that environment, the "doing executive" can make refinements, adjustments, and improvements continuously within the parameters set by the "knowing" and "being" executives.

As your thinking develops about these three steps in the cycle, you seek confirmation from experts in the field to make sure that you're not oversimplifying or miscategorizing fundamental differences in style and preferences. With the help of your outside consultant Eric Marchant and other experts in organizational behavior and clinical psychology, you conclude that the basic characteristics of knowing, being, and doing inform the lives of every human being, but one characteristic tends to play a dominant role in a given individual's outlook, while the other two remain somewhat latent. With respect to the Myers-Briggs type categories, "knowing" executives are NTs (intuitive and thinking), while "being" executives are NFs (intuitive and feeling), and "doing" executives are SJs (sensing and judging) or SPs (sensing and perceiving). According to Myers-Briggs, approximately 70 percent of the population identifies themselves as "doers" while the other 30 percent splits evenly between "knowers" and "be-ers."

In the midst of your efforts to confirm your theory about the three-step cycle, your son, who's studying American literature at Harvard, draws your attention to Ralph Waldo Emerson's "The Poet," which describes three children of the universe who appear in all literature, namely, "the knower, the sayer, and the doer." According to Emerson, the knower or sage searches for truth, while the sayer or poet searches for beauty, and the doer or hero searches for good. Immediately the parallel between your own theory and Emerson's becomes clear, causing you to probe more deeply into Emerson's description of the sayer, only to discover that the sayer represents a communicator, articulator, or persuader, one who looks for integrating ideas that capture wholeness. You recognize the sayer as a "being" executive who serves as culture builder in organizational life.

As your confidence in your three-step cycle grows, you prepare to launch it companywide to drive shifts in assignments, situation analyses, and general management techniques throughout FaraCom. To accomplish this, you develop three possible options for proceeding: an aggressive all-

out focus on the three-step cycle, a more balanced and tempered implementation designed to avoid initially inappropriate extremes, or a cautious
and limited application aimed at eliminating any possible abuses. To evaluate the three options, you create a $3'' \times 3''$ grid and rank the options from
1 to 3 (1 represents the best) in three categories: maximizing customer satisfaction, maximizing employee satisfaction, and maximizing productivity.

	Maximizing Customer Satisfaction	Maximizing Employee Satisfaction	Maximizing Productivity
Aggressive implementation	2	3	1
Balanced implementation	1	2	2
Cautious implementation	3	1	3

When you ask for input from your division presidents, they disagree
about the proper emphasis. It all boils down to which evaluation criterion
you think should take precedence over the other two. Implementation mis-
takes at this stage could hinder future progress or even destroy everything
you've built to date. Now the time has come for you to make a decision.

---

*If you choose to pursue an all-out, aggressive implementation of the
three-step cycle, turn to Chapter 46, page 171.*

*If you prefer a balanced and tempered approach, turn to Chapter 47,
page 173.*

*If you think a cautious and limited program will work best, turn to
Chapter 48, page 175.*

CHAPTER 30

Taking the Three Fields of Work to the Next Level

Your fourth year as CEO of FaraCom brings great satisfaction as you watch your seven division presidents achieve dramatic improvements in their productivity simply by paying attention to the three fields of work: completing, unifying, and magnifying. For all of you, planning a day's activities begins with considering which field of work needs emphasis. In a highly motivational management meeting, Mona Sork, president of retail operations, relates a story that captures how focusing on the three fields of work has helped all of your divisions. She recounts her own experience: "I'm used to living in the completing work field because it's easy for me and I think I'm pretty good at it. However, focusing on the three fields of work has forced me out of my comfort zone, which has been scary, but exciting. A month ago I held a meeting with my managers during which we focused only on magnifying work. We wanted to discover some new insights about our business so we could create more value for our customers. Four hours later, we experienced a major breakthrough. We realized for the first time that customers come to our stores seeking entertainment, not just to buy books, tapes, videos and software that entertain. They consider browsing in our stores in the same category as watching a movie, eating out, attending a concert, or going to a party. We've already confirmed our new insights in a telephone survey. Now, we are moving ahead with plans to revamp store layouts, add espresso bars, and increase the number of chairs and tables. We already know that sales increase based on two factors: number of customers and length of visit. Our new approach will increase both, and we expect it to increase sales by 25 percent within three months. All this because I decided to leave my comfort zone and enter a field of work I naturally neglect. Applying the three fields of work accomplishes two things: (1) it makes you much more conscious of the kind of work you do daily, weekly, and monthly; and (2) it keeps you well rounded and balanced, better enabling you to maintain productivity in all three fields."

The rest of your division presidents summarize their feelings. Sean Cope, president of cable television operations, says, "I've never spent so much time thinking about how and why I work. It's made a huge difference in my life." Alan Peay admits: "I spend more time thinking about unifying and magnifying work than I ever would have without this framework." David Zollweg offers a different point of view: "My problem has always been not paying enough attention to the details of execution and implementation. The three-fields-of-work framework gives me the tool I need to link all three together. My wife's even noticed a big difference." Janice Kofoed, president of catalog sales and direct marketing, exclaims, "I've never paid attention to planning my day, my week, or my month. It's just sort of happened for me, but now I actually relish planning my activities to make sure I'm spending quality time in all three fields." Stephen Ferreira, president of film and video production, observes: "I'm actually sleeping better. I don't worry as much. I feel more contentment and satisfaction in my work. I know it's because I feel more whole and integrated in everything I'm doing." Lisa Harshaw, president of book publishing, echoes Ferreira's feelings: "These three fields of work have done more to help me feel like a whole person than any other approach to planning, scheduling, or prioritizing my life." Even Bill Faragut notices the difference among your seven division presidents and observes, at the March board meeting, that you seem to have found a way to develop the "whole" executive.

As the months roll on, you take the concept of the three fields of work to the next level of management, deploying the division presidents as team leaders for their respective management groups to help that next level of management apply the concept of always working in three fields of endeavor. Once again, you see dramatic increases in productivity as the next level of management begins making better decisions, expanding the context of their decision making to include the consideration of more alternatives and implications. The quality of decision making, both strategic and operational, climbs to a new level throughout FaraCom.

By the end of your fourth year as CEO, revenues pass well beyond the billion dollar mark, with profits climbing to over $100 million, as shown below:

Selected Financial and Productivity Information
(Revenues and Profits in $ Millions)

	Fourth Year	Third Year
Revenues	$1,221	$841
Profits	123	61
Employees	2,451	1,829
Revenues per Employee (Actual $)	$498,164	$459,814
Profits per Employee (Actual $)	$50,184	$33,352

At the beginning of your fifth year as CEO, you face another decision. Should you execute a formal companywide roll-out of the three fields of work, should you let the concept spread informally from middle management to others in the organization, or should you continue concentrating on building the productivity of your seven division presidents? As you wrestle with these three options, you summarize your thinking in a 3" × 3" matrix, ranking each option from 1 to 3 (1 represents the best):

	Maximizing the Productivity of Your Seven Division Presidents	Maximizing the Productivity of Middle Management	Maximizing the Productivity of All Employees
A companywide roll-out	3	3	1
Informal spreading of the word	2	1	2
Concentrating on the division presidents	1	2	3

As so often happens, the decision depends on which goal attracts you the most: maximizing the productivity of your division presidents, your middle managers, or all your people. To this point you have worked on building the productivity of your seven division presidents, but you now see merit in shifting your effort to the entire organization. Which way will you go?

If you decide to execute a formal companywide roll-out of the three fields of work, turn to Chapter 49, page 177.

If you choose an informal spreading of the word throughout the organization, turn to Chapter 50, page 181.

If you want to concentrate on building the productivity of your seven division presidents, turn to Chapter 51, page 185.

Chapter 31

Holding Firm to Time Management

While you know Bill Faragut feels unhappy about your performance to date and believes that FaraCom should have come further by now under your leadership, you believe you could have accomplished little more, given the company's plight when you arrived. Nonetheless, you feel compelled to do something because Faragut still calls the shots as chairman of the board and majority stockholder.

Augmenting your concern, Stephen Ferreira, president of film and video production, steps into your office and closes the door. "Faragut cornered me last night after the screening of our latest Field Trip video. He thinks you're obsessing on time management. Thought you ought to know."

"What do you think?"

"The time management stuff has been helpful, but it may have delivered all the improvement it can."

"Where do we go from here?"

"That's your call. I've gotten my hands full with an overly ambitious production schedule."

To deal with the mounting pressure, you join a group called the "Executive Forum," which brings together CEOs from around the country to discuss problems and exchange ideas. You've given up trying to talk to Bill Faragut about the situation because whenever you begin to explore alternatives with him, he obviously considers that a sign of weakness and tells you to think it through yourself. You're hoping that the Executive

Forum will provide an outlet for your frustration as well as a source of ideas for building productivity at FaraCom.

The Forum meets once a month for a four-hour session, beginning in the morning and ending after lunch. After three meetings, you know the investment of $5,000 in annual fees will prove worthwhile because you can already see where you want to take FaraCom in the future. Long and penetrating discussions with CEOs of other companies have made it clear to you that while better time management really can benefit your organization and its people, it can only go so far in terms of productivity. Having reached the point where most people have fairly well mastered time management, you must prepare to move beyond it. Luckily, three other Forum members faced a similar problem and successfully addressed it by redirecting their focus on productivity planning and evaluation. With the help of your newfound colleagues, you begin weighing various options for the next stage of productivity improvement at FaraCom.

By year end, you've identified your options, but you'll have to move quickly because you know Bill Faragut finds the results lackluster. Revenues increase to $800 million, with profits climbing to $18 million, as shown below:

Selected Financial and Productivity Information
(Revenues and Profits in $ Millions)

	Fourth Year	*Third Year*
Revenues	$802	$719
Profits	18	6
Employees	2,001	1,938
Revenues per Employee (Actual $)	$400,799	$371,001
Profits per Employee (Actual $)	$8,996	$3,096

With your fourth year as CEO behind you, you contemplate the three options you've identified for moving beyond time management: adopt a companywide employee productivity planning and evaluation program, put your division managers through an intensive off-site productivity improvement course, or reorganize the company to create a more productive work environment.

To summarize your thoughts and feelings, you create a 3″ × 3″ matrix in which you rank each of these options from 1 to 3 (1 representing the best):

	Maximizing Individual Productivity	Maximizing Team Productivity	Maximizing Organizational Productivity
Adopting an employee productivity program	1	2	2
Sending executives to an off-site productivity workshop	2	1	3
Reorganizing for a better environment to promote productivity	3	3	1

Although you see pros and cons down each path, you can also see that your decision boils down to your own particular preference. Which goal should you shoot for first: stronger individual, team, or organizational productivity?

With little time to lose, you must implement this decision within a few weeks.

If you decide to adopt the employee productivity program, turn to Chapter 52, page 189.

If you want to send your executives to a productivity workshop, turn to Chapter 53, page 193.

If you would rather reorganize the company to create a more productive environment, turn to Chapter 54, page 197.

CHAPTER 32

Taking First Things First, a Second Step

Basking in the warm glow of last year's results, you begin thinking about how to extend the message of "principles over procedures" throughout FaraCom. As you look for ways to enhance the principled-centered view, your commitment to organizationwide productivity continues to guide your thinking. To take the next step, you draw from Covey's *First Things First* several kernels of truth for distribution throughout the organization:

- The enemy of the "best" is the "good."
- Anything less than a conscious commitment to the important is an unconscious commitment to the unimportant.
- Doing more things faster is no substitute for doing the right things.
- It's easy to say "no!" when there's a deeper "yes!" burning inside.
- You can want to do the right thing, and you can even want to do it for the right reasons. But if you don't apply the right principles, you can still hit a wall.
- Quality of life depends on what happens in the space between stimulus and response.
- Difference is the beginning of synergy.
- Any time we think the problem is "out there," that thought is the problem.

With such slogans you continue stimulating thought throughout the organization about principles and priorities, always stressing what Covey calls the fourth generation of time and life management: to live, to love, to learn, and to leave a legacy, based on the four basic endowments of self-awareness, conscience, creative imagination, and independent will.

In a one-on-one session with you, David Zollweg, president of software and CD-ROM publishing, admits, "Two years ago I would have called all this stuff we've been doing a lot of vague and fuzzy mumbo-jumbo, but the Covey principles have had a huge impact on my division. Because of principles such as 'seek first to understand,' we see conflict as healthy. It brings ideas to our attention that we may not want to hear, but that may be the answers to our problems. There's no question that we're increasing productivity."

All these efforts keep your organization moving in the right direction during your fourth year as CEO, and most of the feedback you receive confirms that people everywhere in the company are internalizing the idea of putting first things first and living by fundamental principles. Stephen Ferreira, president of film and video production, tells you how his division's commitment to the principle of win-win relationships has led to partnerships with a film crew union that has historically promoted antagonistic relations with management. "We're believers in the power of working by principles," he exclaims.

When your fourth year comes to a close, sales climb to just over $1 billion, with profits soaring to $130 million, as shown below:

Selected Financial and Productivity Information
(Revenues and Profits in $ Millions)

	Fourth Year	Third Year
Revenues	$1,009	$835
Profits	131	62
Employees	1,943	1,878
Revenues per Employee (Actual $)	$519,300	$444,622
Profits per Employee (Actual $)	$67,422	$33,014

After the first of the year, however, your division presidents begin lobbying for a new thrust for the coming year. Stephen Ferreira, your president of film and video production, sums it up best when he says, "I think the focus on principles and 'first things first' has provided the philosophical basis for cultural change at FaraCom, but now we need to systematize or institutionalize all this conceptual stuff so it can continue to help us make tangible improvements in productivity." You like the way Ferreira posed the challenge, and you invite everyone to propose new ideas for the coming year.

At the next senior management meeting with your seven division presidents, you ask each of them to sketch a new or revised companywide focus that can systematize and institutionalize the "first things first" and principle-centered behavior. After a great deal of discussion and debate, the team boils the suggestions down to the three most attractive alternatives: (1) helping people to make better principle-centered choices everyday, (2) assisting people to better evaluate their activities on a daily basis as the key to learning, or (3) building win-win stewardship agreements with every employee.

As you wrestle with these options and continue exploring their consequences with your seven division presidents, you summarize their preferences, your own thinking, and input from Bill Faragut in the following $3'' \times 3''$ matrix, which ranks each option from 1 to 3 in terms of maximizing productivity, results, or the future viability of the company (1 signifies the best):

	Maximizing Productivity	*Maximizing Results*	*Maximizing Future Viability of the Company*
Helping people learn how to make better principle-centered choices	1	3	1
Assisting people better evaluate their activities to increase learning	2	2	3
Building win-win stewardship agreements	3	1	2

Which goal motivates you the most: maximize productivity, maximize results, or maximize future viability? Now you must act quickly. What will you do?

If you decide to focus on helping people make better principle-centered choices, turn to Chapter 55, page 201.

If you want to help employees better evaluate their activities in order to maximize learning, turn to Chapter 56, page 205.

If you believe that building win-win stewardship agreements between individuals in the company will work best, turn to Chapter 57, page 209.

CHAPTER 33

Cruising the FaraNet

As a result of intense employee training during the first three months of your fourth year as CEO, FaraCom makes a major breakthrough with the help of EmpowerTech consultants and trainers by substantially strengthening the company's communications network (FaraNet). FaraNet allows for the downloading of software from company libraries, depositing and retrieving messages on bulletin boards, participating in real-time conferences, and contributing to an unlimited number of roundtables. You also open FaraNet to your customers, offering them free 24-hour access as part of a program that provides product discounts, special service offerings, and round-the-clock interaction with the company.

FaraNet expands rapidly as more than 40 percent of the company's customers link up to provide feedback, state preferences regarding products and services, and exponentially increase the amount of communication with FaraCom employees. Much to the surprise of Janice Kofoed, president of catalog sales and direct marketing, nearly 60 percent of her division's five million preferred customers link up with FaraNet to place product orders, provide feedback on products, and participate in product testing and research over a three month period. She sums up the feelings of all seven division presidents, "The number of people on the FaraNet astonishes me. Things have moved much faster than I ever expected. Luckily, we had enough foresight to invest in technology and software early."

Internally, employees throughout the organization eagerly seize the opportunity to use real-time conferencing and roundtables to discuss issues, resolve problems, tap under-utilized talents and resources, and generally maximize their productivity. Though just one of more than 50,000 corporate research and educational networks that comprise the worldwide Internet or so-called information superhighway, FaraNet quickly becomes the leading one in the communications and entertainment industry, enabling the company to enter into a host of alliances with others in the industry to offer products ranging from books and magazines to videos and software to an ever expanding customer base.

Before long, FaraNet roundtables include science fiction, gourmet food, the White House, comics, photography, travel, military, religion, motorcycles, daytime television, dogs, cats, genealogy, recipes, current affairs, small business, writers, sports, and a lot more. FaraNet also becomes a clearinghouse for ideas about scripts for movies, architecture for software, ideas for CD-ROM, book proposals, and magazine articles, and it stimulates a wealth of customer opinion, giving FaraCom a preemptory first shot at meeting customer desires by producing or contracting for products ranging from books and videos to software and CD-ROMs to information and customized reports. E-mail on the FaraNet soars as the company begins providing a service that summarizes customer opinion for other communications and entertainment companies. To manage all this, you establish a new division called FaraNet Services, under the direction of former Time Warner vice president Pete Rozinsky, that pulls in more than $100 million in revenues by the end of the year.

Mona Sork, president of the retail operations, adds a new QVC-type television cable network to her division with the help of Sean Cope, president of cable television operations, which allows customers to purchase a wide variety of communications and entertainment related products interactively. She comments, "EmpowerTech has changed my life. I never use the phone anymore. All my communications are on E-mail or through on-line conferences and roundtables. It's not science fiction, it's science reality."

Ultimately, near the end of your fourth year as CEO of FaraCom, you see clearly that the FaraNet provides a much better way to match buyer's desires and seller's offerings. Just before the end of the year, FaraCom launches an on-line catalog of the widest array of books, magazines, videos, software, and CD-ROM products available anywhere in the world. Its inauguration hits the front page of every major newspaper in the United States and many throughout the world, as customers from as far away as China can access the easy-to-peruse FaraNet directory of communications and entertainment products, order a product instantly on the screen, and receive it by DHL, for a low shipping charge of $3, the next day.

At year end, sales jump to $1.3 billion and profits soar to $200 million, as shown below:

Selected Financial and Productivity Information
(Revenues and Profits in $ Millions)

	Fourth Year	Third Year
Revenues	$1,338	$769
Profits	199	31
Employees	2,978	1,958
Revenues per Employee (Actual $)	$449,295	$392,748
Profits per Employee (Actual $)	$66,823	$15,832

At the beginning of your fifth year as CEO of FaraCom, your biggest problem has become managing growth. FaraNet, now a household name, takes 25 million customer orders during the first quarter alone, creating a problem you define as "megagrowth." With over a thousand new employees and almost double the revenues, FaraCom operations sizzle with activity and face a variety of new challenges: insufficient office space, a growing number of telecommuters, limited growth capital, overloaded managers, inadequate entry-level training programs, and the general inability to exploit a growing number of opportunities.

After a lot of brainstorming with your eight division presidents (including new FaraNet Services division president Pete Rozinsky) and Bill Faragut, you realize that no one sees the full vision of possibilities as well as you do. Not even the visionary Faragut can comprehend the extent of the opportunity FaraNet has created. You realize you must push the board to take the company public sometime this year, but if you can't quickly resolve the company's megagrowth problems, FaraCom can easily lose the lead it has captured in the Internet world.

Your choices come down to three major possibilities: split out FaraNet as a separate company and take it public immediately, keep the company together and promote synergy between the divisions, or accept a recent offer from QVC to merge.

As you consider these three options and their potential impact on productivity, growth and profit, you create a 3″ × 3″ matrix ranking the possibilities from 1 to 3 (1 represents the best):

	Maximize Productivity	Maximize Growth	Maximize Profit
Split out FaraNet	1	2	2
Remain integrated	3	3	1
Merge with QVC	2	1	3

Which goal should you set first: maximizing productivity, growth, or profits?

Without a second to waste, you must make this move decisively. What will you do?

If you decide to split out FaraNet as a separate public company, turn to Chapter 58, page 213.

If you want to maintain one company and emphasize the synergy between divisions, turn to Chapter 59, page 217.

If you choose to merge with QVC, turn to Chapter 60, page 219.

CHAPTER 34

Staying at FaraCom for the Long Haul

After a long and sleepless night contemplating your future, you decide to stay at FaraCom to continue building the world's best values-based communications and entertainment company. Bill Faragut congratulates you on making the right decision, and together you begin laying the groundwork for an initial public offering (IPO) later in the year.

With Goldman Sachs on board to structure and underwrite the IPO, you turn your attention to strengthening FaraCom's position. Once again, you use "maximizing your own productivity" as the guiding principle for your preparation and planning because you've come to realize that when you do so everything else seems to fall into place automatically. During an in-depth interview with a *Forbes* magazine reporter, you explain your philosophy, "As far as I'm concerned, every individual in an organization is unique and can make a unique contribution. Whether someone actually makes that contribution depends on how well that person has learned to maximize his or her own productivity. At FaraCom we find people with the talents we need and then provide an environment where they can flourish and grow. And, I'm no different from anyone else. I look first and foremost at my own productivity, because that ultimately enables me to help others do the same."

Within a few short weeks, you set out a four-point plan of action for yourself and the company: First, you hire Ketchum Public Relations to promote FaraCom's image and reputation as the undisputed leader in the "val-

141

ues revolution." With so much to work with in terms of interesting people and bold, new products, Ketchum easily keeps FaraCom in the limelight week after week. Stories about FaraCom's "Decisions" video series, which highlights great value-creating decisions in history, a new family values television cable channel, and the expanding series of values-based books and software find their way into magazines, newspapers, TV news programs, and information networks on a regular basis.

Second, you engage The Hay Group, a consulting firm, to design a set of "golden handcuffs" for each of your division presidents that will make staying with the company much more financially attractive than leaving, no matter how lucrative the offers. You know that three of your six existing division presidents, Janice Kofoed, David Zollweg, and Lisa Harshaw (Mona Sork departed with the retail operation), have received attractive offers from competing firms. You are thankful that they decided to stay after you assured them you yourself were staying, but you know the temptation to leave will only grow as offers become more irresistible.

Third, you ask the Ernst & Young consultants to begin an exhaustive search for acquisition, alliance, or affiliation candidates that could fit under FaraCom's values-based umbrella. You and Bill Faragut agree that FaraCom's success to date and all the media exposure puts it in an excellent position to acquire or affiliate with other similarly oriented companies. You describe FaraCom's position to the Ernst & Young team as "strategic opportunism," making clear to them that you want FaraCom to become a strategic magnet for values-based communications and entertainment companies.

Finally, in late March, you take your six division presidents to Naples, Florida, for a three-day retreat, during which you devise an innovative strategy to package book, film, CD, software, magazine, and television projects around historical turning points of pure inspiration, visionary enlightenment, or courageous action that have produced the world's greatest contributions. Each project would include a bundle of products such as biographies, magazine articles, television programs, movies, CDs, and software. These projects might include figures such as Petrarch, the Renaissance scholar and poet, whose fascination with the link between classical Greek-Roman mythology and Christianity inspired his early mystical experiences; Sir Isaac Newton, an architect of the scientific revolution, who credits a power greater than himself for enlightening his mind about gravity, light, and mathematics; Johann Wolfgang von Goethe, the renowned German author, who cites his "golden mean," the blending of two opposite strains, his mother's wild imagination and his father's methodical steadiness, as the source of his genius; Wolfgang Amadeus Mozart, perhaps the greatest musical genius of all time, who claimed to have seen visions of fully completed musical works flowing before his senses; or Albert Einstein, undoubtedly one of the greatest thinkers in history, who admits to meditating on God to construct the theoretical leaps that led to entirely new ways of thinking about time, space, matter, energy, and gravity.

In the months that follow, you successfully complete your first public offering of 14 million shares of Class A Common Stock, raising $230 million in equity financing to reduce debt and fund future growth. By year end, the Ernst & Young consultants help you obtain three acquisitions: Home Entertainment, a family-oriented CD-ROM development company; *Readers Digest*, the American mainstream monthly magazine; and CastleRock, a film studio and production company. Your six division presidents receive attractive stock-option packages, which firmly lock them into FaraCom's future. And, most significantly, you introduce your first two *Moments in History* packages on Mozart and Einstein to rave reviews and combined sales of $130 million in six months.

At the end of your fifth year as CEO of FaraCom, the company records revenues of $2 billion, including the revenues of the acquired companies, and profits of $250 million, as shown below:

Selected Financial and Productivity Information
(Revenues and Profits in $ Millions)

	Fifth Year	*Fourth Year*
Revenues	$2,012	$1,003
Profits	253	101
Employees	4,211	2,008
Revenues per Employee (Actual $)	$477,796	$499,501
Profits per Employee (Actual $)	$60,081	$50,299

This marks the end of your decision making at FaraCom. The company's and your future look bright because you have tenaciously worked to improve and maximize your own productivity. *The Productivity Game* doesn't end here, however. You can continue studying ways to improve productivity by pursuing one of the following options.

To find out how your choices stack up against the other possibilities, turn to Chapter 61, A Ranking of the Outcomes, page 221.

To review the other choices you could have made at the last decision point, turn to Chapters 35 and 36, pages 145 and 147.

To embark on another decision-making track that focuses on maximizing personal productivity, turn to Chapter 6, Developing Strong Divisional Strategies and Cultures, page 29.

To embark on a decision-making track that focuses on building the productivity of your seven division presidents, turn to Chapter 3, Increasing the Productivity of Division Presidents, page 15.

CHAPTER 35

Moving to Viacom-Paramount

After tossing and turning all night, you finally decide to accept Viacom-Paramount's offer to become CEO of the $20 billion enterprise. Bill Faragut insists that you're making a big mistake, but you remain convinced that you can do more good for the growing values movement at Viacom-Paramount than you can at FaraCom or at Ernst & Young.

After recommending Janice Kofoed become the new CEO of FaraCom, you quickly begin making the transition, in order to assume your new responsibilities at Viacom-Paramount within the next 60 days. After two weeks of silence, Bill Faragut finally warms up again and asks you to serve as a member of FaraCom's board of directors. You gain the necessary approvals from the Viacom-Paramount board, hoping to provide continued assistance to Kofoed as she assumes control of your old company.

Over the next several months you direct your attention toward building a cohesive strategy at Viacom-Paramount that tunes in to the values movement and pulls all the diverse operations within the company under an overarching vision of creating products and services for a values generation. Success comes quickly as various Viacom-Paramount divisions respond favorably to the united vision and you jettison operations that cannot implement the strategy or cannot attain leadership in their market or industry. Within six months you sell off two scientific textbook divisions, three film and video-related operations, one professional sports franchise, four retail operations, two television stations, and a dozen other unrelated businesses.

At the same time, you remain close to FaraCom when you give guidance to Janice Kofoed at the four board meetings during the year, communicating to her what you would have done if you had remained on as CEO: take the company public; expand through acquisitions; revise the compensation program to keep FaraCom's best people; and take the integrated strategy one step further by launching packages of products drawn from each of the divisions. Janice adopts most of your plans and continues the spirit of your leadership at FaraCom, taking the company to $1.4 billion in what would have been your fifth year had you remained there as CEO.

In an interview with the press, Kofoed attributes much of FaraCom's success to your consistent application of a unified strategic theme within the company, an approach she has steadfastly continued in your absence. You, in turn, give her full credit for FaraCom's continued growth and success, chalking up the past year's success to her ability to maintain continuity while at the same time adding her own unique contributions.

While this outcome proved positive for you personally, you concluded your decision making at FaraCom when you left for Viacom-Paramount. However, you can try your hand at productivity improvement again by pursuing one of the options below.

To find out how this outcome compares to other possibilities, turn to Chapter 61, A Ranking of the Outcomes, page 221.

To review the other choices you could have pursued at the last decision point, turn to Chapters 34 and 36, pages 141 and 147.

To embark on another decision-making track that focuses on maximizing personal productivity, turn to Chapter 6, Developing Strong Divisional Strategies and Cultures, page 29.

To pursue a decision-making track that focuses on building the productivity of your seven division presidents, turn to Chapter 3, Increasing the Productivity of Division Presidents, page 15.

CHAPTER 36

Returning to Ernst & Young as a Managing Partner

Unable to sleep until 4:00 A.M., you finally decide to return to Ernst & Young as managing partner overseeing the consulting operation. Bill Faragut laments your decision but decides that, for the benefit of FaraCom, the Ernst & Young assignment will at least allow you to continue helping the company over the next couple of years. You quickly develop transition plans and recommend that Stephen Ferreira assume the reins at FaraCom. The board agrees.

You work out a reasonable contractual arrangement with Bill Faragut to remain on as a consultant with the latitude to assign other Ernst & Young project teams to help take FaraCom public in the coming year, make additional acquisitions, strengthen the compensation incentives for key executives, and push the integrated strategy to the next step.

Your new assignment at Ernst & Young proves extremely challenging as you revamp the entire consulting operation under a new unified strategy that focuses on strategy execution, still a major void in the consulting marketplace. Your new rallying cry for Ernst & Young consulting becomes a strong motivator for offices throughout the United States and the world, as you pull the best minds into the company on a temporary basis to design the basic principles, guidelines, and consulting methodologies for an emphasis on strategy execution.

Within your first year as managing partner at Ernst & Young, you're able to link most consulting assignments to a strategy execution focus, which earns the company a vibrant new image in the marketplace. Even the most technical or mundane projects, such as reconfiguring a management information system, streamlining customer service operations, or establishing new financial controls, begin with a clarification of the organization's strategy and an assessment of how that strategy should influence the project. At the end of your first year, consulting revenues increase by 25 percent to $1 billion. Once again, you discover that maximizing your own productivity leads to extraordinary success.

At the same time, you have helped FaraCom's Stephen Ferreira through a number of consulting projects during the year that focus on getting the company ready for its initial public offering, redesigning its compensation package for key executives, identifying acquisition candidates, and developing a strategy that pulls products from each of the divisions into a packaged offering of books, videos, television programs, magazine ideas, and so forth. At year end, the revenues at FaraCom reach $1.3 billion.

Of course, you ended your decision making at FaraCom when you returned to Ernst & Young. However, you can continue playing *The Productivity Game* by selecting one of the options below.

To see how this outcome compares to other possibilities, turn to Chapter 61, A Ranking of the Outcomes, page 221.

To review the other choices you could have made at the last decision point, turn to Chapters 34 and 35, pages 141 and 145.

To embark on another decision-making track that focuses on maximizing personal productivity, turn to Chapter 6, Developing Strong Divisional Strategies and Cultures, page 29.

To pursue a decision-making track that aims at building the productivity of your seven division presidents, turn to Chapter 3, Increasing the Productivity of Division Presidents, page 15.

CHAPTER 37

Emphasizing External Acquisitions

In light of the success of the recent spin-outs and the acquisition of six new companies, you believe your greatest contribution to FaraCom will come from bringing the right additional acquisitions under FaraCom's umbrella. Bill Faragut reluctantly agrees with your plan and recommends that the board of directors give preliminary approval for at least 6 acquisitions in the coming year.

When one member of the board questions the company's ability to assimilate 6 more companies, you make a strong case that maximizing change can best maximize productivity throughout the company. You cite Jack Welch of General Electric, who, at the end of his tenure as CEO, expressed only one regret: namely, that he had moved too slowly. He wished he had effected more change earlier. You argue that the three tenets now entrenched in FaraCom's culture—innovative leadership, market dominance, and radical improvement—can do nothing but grow stronger in the midst of continuous change and continuous acquisitions.

Over the next several months, you implement your strategy, working hard to identify the best acquisition candidates for FaraCom. As you proceed, you feel somewhat uncomfortable about the application of your skills and talents. You have never been that successful at external acquisitions or deal making, and you know from experience that your core talents lie in developing internal strategies and cultures. Even though you wonder whether you've made the right decision, you conclude that this move will enhance your own personal growth, and you fully expect your own productivity to expand as a result.

Midway through the year, it becomes apparent that FaraCom has overextended itself with its acquisitions. With only three acquisitions completed and the company's debt burgeoning rapidly—$300 million in new long-term corporate bonds—Bill Faragut calls you into his office to tell you he's considering selling the company.

The news stuns you. "Why?"

He shakes his head sadly. "Because I'm not comfortable with the debt we've accumulated in the past few months."

"It's only temporary," you respond.

"Maybe, but I wasn't cut out for this kind of high corporate finance. I can't sleep at night. I'm miserable."

You leave Faragut's office bewildered and depressed. Should you have focused more on shoring up the internal strategies and cultures of the spin-out companies and the already acquired companies? Doing so might have kept Bill Faragut happy. Have you misapplied your own talents and capabilities? Maybe so.

Still convinced you can get Bill Faragut to change his mind, you decide to focus attention on improving the productivity of the individual operations under the FaraCom umbrella. However, three weeks later, Bill Faragut informs you that he has reached an agreement in principle to sell FaraCom to General Electric. Faragut also tells you that you will not be part of the deal and should start looking for another job. Six months short of completing five years as CEO of FaraCom, you find yourself out of work, albeit with an attractive severance package—three years of salary—that will give you plenty of time to look around.

This marks the end of your decision making on this track, but you can continue to play *The Productivity Game* by pursuing one of the options below.

If you want to see how this outcome compares to other possibilities, turn to Chapter 61, A Ranking of the Outcomes, page 221.

If you want to review the other choices you could have made at your last decision-making point, turn to Chapters 38 and 39, pages 151 and 153.

If you want to embark on another decision-making track that focuses on maximizing personal productivity, turn to Chapter 7, Training Your Seven Division Presidents to Think Strategically, page 33.

If you would prefer moving onto a new decision-making track that aims at building the productivity of your seven division presidents, turn to Chapter 3, Increasing the Productivity of Division Presidents, page 15.

CHAPTER 38

Directing Your Energies Internally to Build Strategies and Cultures

Your emphasis on maximizing your own personal productivity has paid off once again as you have taken full advantage of your own talents and capabilities by building the strategies and cultures of each of the acquired and spun-out companies. Paying strict attention to self-deployment has served you well. You now oversee 13 companies in the FaraCom family, all of which you intend to strengthen both strategically and culturally. You ask David Zollweg, president of software and CD-ROM publishing, to assume the additional responsibilities of executive vice president of FaraCom with the specific charge to oversee the company's seven original divisions.

You tell Bill Faragut that you're going to put all acquisitions on hold for the next 12 months to ensure the successful growth and development of what you've built so far. He applauds your decision, arguing that it's the only way to make sure that FaraCom will move solidly into the future. By spending individual time with each of the presidents of the six new acquisitions over the first three months of your fifth year as CEO, you avoid a lot of problems that could have otherwise caused great difficulty.

You make it possible for Media Play to grow from 60 to 90 stores, you help negotiate deals with 10 major news magazines to become part of the Magavision group, and you push Interactive Films to redirect its strategy by renting out CD-ROM players and discs through Family Favorites and Blockbuster Video.

151

By year end, sales increase to $1.4 billion, as shown below:

Selected Financial and Productivity Information
(Revenues and Profits in $ Millions)

	Fifth Year	Fourth Year
Revenues	$1,389	$1,104
Profits	111	63
Employees	2,772	2,276
Revenues per Employee (Actual $)	$501,082	$485,062
Profits per Employee (Actual $)	$40,043	$27,680

As you look back at your five years as CEO of FaraCom, you take pride in the results you've achieved by building strong strategies and cultures in each of the FaraCom entities. Now the company seems poised for even more spectacular growth as you launch a new wave of acquisitions in the coming year and hope to double and even triple revenues within the next two years.

This concludes your decision making at FaraCom, but you can continue playing *The Productivity Game* by choosing one of the options below.

If you want to see how your decision making stacks up against other possible outcomes, turn to Chapter 61, A Ranking of the Outcomes, page 221.

If you want to review the other choices you could have made at your last decision making point, turn to Chapters 37 and 39, pages 149 and 153.

If you desire to embark upon a different decision-making track that focuses on maximizing personal productivity, turn to Chapter 7, Training Your Seven Division Presidents to Think Strategically, page 33.

If you prefer pursuing a decision-making track that builds productivity among your seven presidents, turn to Chapter 3, Increasing the Productivity of Division Presidents, page 15.

CHAPTER 39

Acquiring NBC

Enraptured with the opportunity to acquire NBC and flattered by General Electric's scrutiny of your operating style over the last several months, you undertake a penetrating analysis of network television, spending every day of the first six months of your fifth year as CEO of FaraCom making the NBC acquisition. The investment necessary to reposition NBC with a strategy to support cable operations and provide programming outside the network puts FaraCom into heavy debt, demanding an initial public offering within a few months. Unfortunately, another by-product of your intense focus on NBC manifests itself: Some of the other companies within FaraCom begin struggling to maintain growth and profitability. Sean Cope, president of cable television operations, and Stephen Ferreira, president of film and video production, openly rebel against you and your obsession with NBC. They blame you for a growing sense of uncertainty and declining morale in their divisions. In a senior management meeting in August, they both confront you.

"NBC was a mistake," says Cope.

Ferreira adds, "Your total focus on NBC has made everyone in the company wonder about their future. Everyone's talking about your NBC ego trip and your neglect of other FaraCom businesses."

Shocked by the pent-up emotion, you simply say, "NBC was not a mistake, and I expect both of you to quell any vicious rumors."

"Easier said than done," responds Cope.

"I'll talk to each of you individually about this, after the meeting."

153

As you step back to take stock of your situation, you finally acknowledge that NBC's flattery caused you to lose track of your focus on building and maximizing your own productivity. Not only did the NBC deal distract you from what you do best, it exacerbated the debt problem and placed inordinate pressure on the company to go to the equity market prematurely for increased funding.

Three months before completing your fifth year as CEO of FaraCom, Bill Faragut asks for your resignation in order to bring in a new CEO from the outside. As it turns out, the investment bankers you hired recommended your termination.

This brings an end to your decision making at FaraCom, but you can continue playing the game by choosing one of the options below.

If you want to see how this outcome compares with other possibilities, turn to Chapter 61, A Ranking of the Outcomes, page 221.

If you want to review the choices you could have made in your last decision, turn to Chapters 37 and 38, pages 149 and 151.

If you would like to embark on another decision-making track that focuses on maximizing personal productivity, turn to Chapter 7, Training Your Seven Division Presidents to Think Strategically, page 33.

If you prefer pursuing a path that focuses on building productivity of your seven division presidents, turn to Chapter 3, Increasing the Productivity of Division Presidents, page 15.

CHAPTER 40

Downsizing FaraCom

Convinced that you can bring about additional productivity improvements at FaraCom only by downsizing every division's operations, you hire a downsizing team from Booz Allen to make recommendations for each of FaraCom's divisions. Within three short months, the Booz Allen team recommends a 20 percent cut in personnel across the board and the elimination of several duplicative functions across the divisions. For instance, they suggest combining all finance and accounting, management information, human resource, and public relations functions that now operate independently in the divisions into companywide departments. They also suggest sharing certain R&D and marketing activities among the divisions. By the end of the year, you're able to implement all the recommendations from the downsizing team to improve profits to $12 million on sales of $702 million, as shown below:

Selected Financial and Productivity Information
(Revenues and Profits in $ Millions)

	Fourth Year	*Third Year*
Revenues	$702	$648
Profits	12	.2
Employees	1,995	1,963
Revenues per Employee (Actual $)	$351,880	$330,107
Profits per Employee (Actual $)	$6,015	$102

Unfortunately, the downsizing continues to compromise company growth, and your division presidents complain that the downsizing initiatives have seriously hampered their ability to meet targeted projections in the coming year.

Lisa Harshaw, president of book publishing, sums up the feelings of your seven presidents, "You have attempted to make up for several years of mediocre productivity gains in one precipitous move. In reality, you've only created a lot of human misery and seriously compromised our operations."

Fed up with FaraCom's lackluster performance and your poor decision making, Bill Faragut fires you at the beginning of your fifth year at FaraCom.

Your decision making at FaraCom has come to an abrupt end. However, you can continue playing *The Productivity Game* by choosing one of the following options.

If you want to see how this outcome compares with other possibilities, turn to Chapter 61, A Ranking of the Outcomes, page 221.

If you want to find out what happened with the other choices at your last decision-making point, turn to Chapters 41 and 42, pages 157 and 159.

If you would rather embark on another decision-making track that focuses on maximizing personal productivity, turn to Chapter 5, Creating an Integrated Strategy and Theme, page 25.

If you decide to shift to a totally different decision-making track that focuses on building productivity in your seven division presidents, turn to Chapter 3, Increasing the Productivity of Division Presidents, page 15.

CHAPTER 41

Initiating an Employee Buy-Out

Because you believe Bill Faragut has overreacted to FaraCom's current lackluster productivity improvements, you decide to maneuver him out of ownership and control. Quietly, but quickly, you share your thinking with your division presidents, and you approach Goldman Sachs and Merrill Lynch in New York to determine their interest in supporting the scheme. After several discussions with the two firms, you decide to go with Merrill Lynch, but the principals involved remind you that Bill Faragut's unwillingness to sell could obviously scuttle the entire plan. However, you remain convinced that your chances of convincing Faragut will be greater if you put the strategy, documentation, and procedures of the offering in place before approaching him. With green lights on all fronts, you lay all the necessary groundwork before communicating anything to Bill Faragut about your intentions to buy the company out from him. You enlist the help of your seven presidents to set the stage with employees regarding the potential buy-out. Only Janice Kofoed expresses reluctance. In a private meeting in your office she informs you, "I think you're making a big mistake by not making Bill Faragut part of this from the beginning. It's going to backfire on you."

By midyear, with all the preparations ready and six of your seven division presidents enthusiastically awaiting the opportunity to become owners of FaraCom, you must finally communicate your intentions to Bill Faragut. In a special meeting away from the office, you walk the chairman through a

painstakingly crafted proposal for the buy-out plan. After two hours of emo-
tionless response and a few benign questions, Faragut fires you on the spot.

Stunned by the response, you insist, "You can't do that."

He laughs. "Sure I can. And to think I trusted you with this company."

That's your last conversation with Bill Faragut before you leave
FaraCom to look for employment elsewhere.

This marks the end of your decision making at FaraCom, but you can
continue playing *The Productivity Game* by selecting one of the options
below.

*If you would like to see how this outcome compares to other possibili-
ties, turn to Chapter 61, A Ranking of the Outcomes, page 221.*

*If you want to discover the results of the other choices you could have
made at your last decision-making point, turn to Chapters 40 and 42,
pages 155 and 159.*

*If you want to embark on another decision-making track that empha-
sizes personal productivity, turn to Chapter 5, Creating an Integrated
Strategy and Theme, page 25.*

*If you want to move onto a different decision-making track directed at
building productivity in your seven division presidents, turn to Chapter
3, Increasing the Productivity of Division Presidents, page 15.*

CHAPTER 42

Conducting a Week-Long Retreat with Your Key Executives

Wishing to share responsibility for greater productivity improvements, you take the top 75 FaraCom executives off site for a full-week retreat during which everyone will discuss exactly what can be done in the few short months before the end of your fourth year as CEO. During the retreat, you lay everything on the table, sparking an honest, straightforward, and candid discussion of FaraCom's position and possible future. You discuss Bill Faragut's demands for productivity improvements, the need for growth in sales and profits, and your personal desire that all the time and energy spent in strategic thinking and strategic management training pay off quickly.

Many people vent a lot of pent-up emotion about your theoretical approach to training, bemoaning the lack of practical application and hands-on assistance in implementing strong strategies in their divisions and business units. Alan Peay, president of magazine publishing, Mona Sork, president of retail operations, and Sean Cope, president of cable television operations, in particular, criticize your lack of practical, hands-on management. Mona Sork echoes Sean Cope's earlier frustration, "You've got to come down out of the clouds and face the details of reality." Arguments and debates escalate as fingers point in every direction at who's to blame for the lack of progress to date. You purposely chose to engage no outside facilitators for this retreat in order to get closer to the 75 executives by the end of the week, but you had not expected such a result.

The session's low point occurs Thursday morning when Peay, Sork, and Cope threaten to resign on the spot. But miraculously, through the kind

159

of catharsis that comes only after a full unburdening of grievances and frustrations, you manage to turn things around by outlining a five-point plan to build revenues, profits, and productivity. By Friday, the plan captures the hearts and minds of every person in attendance. Even the three presidents who threatened to resign admit to a change of heart. Alan Peay captures their sentiment, "I think speaking frankly and candidly has helped all of us face the reality of our situation with a more tempered and balanced frame of mind." The five-point plan that everyone endorses includes:

1. Performance challenges for each and every functional team within FaraCom.
2. A reduction in staff of up to 10 percent in some operations before the end of the year.
3. Development of a new strategy-implementation framework that sets practical guidelines for applying all of the training that's been going on recently.
4. A commitment to increase work hours by as much as 20 percent for the next few months, to get through the crisis.
5. A willingness to get every problem out in the open as quickly as possible by maintaining candid, open-ended discussions throughout the organization.

You feel a breath of fresh air as you return from the week-long retreat because you feel certain your clear-cut plan has captured the hearts and minds of your top people. By the end of your fourth year, sales reach $750 million, as shown below:

Selected Financial and Productivity Information
(Revenues and Profits in $ Millions)

	Fourth Year	*Third Year*
Revenues	$749	$648
Profits	10	.2
Employees	2,002	1,963
Revenues per Employee (Actual $)	$374,126	$330,107
Profits per Employee (Actual $)	$4,995	$102

The pressure to improve productivity continues, but the improvements of the last year have demonstrated to Bill Faragut and the board of directors that you're willing to do whatever it takes to build and grow FaraCom.

During your fifth year as CEO, you augment your five-point program, asking your senior executives to implement a project-team philosophy of work at FaraCom that flattens the organization and shifts the focus of employees from "jobs" to "teams." Employees in every division become members of teams, and job descriptions are replaced with field-of-work descriptions. The change requires a lot of communication, training, and long hours, but the benefits of greater common purpose, shared account-ability, and improved results show up quickly.

While many of your executives grow weary and strained under the added pressure of such a major shift, sales increase to over $900 million with profits improving nicely at the end of your fifth year as CEO, as shown below:

Selected Financial and Productivity Information
(Revenues and Profits in $ Millions)

	Fifth Year	*Fourth Year*
Revenues	$903	$749
Profits	41	10
Employees	2,364	2,002
Revenues per Employee (Actual $)	$381,980	$374,126
Profits per Employee (Actual $)	$17,343	$4,995

While this progress pleases you, you worry that you've only added to the frustration of already overworked people, and you recall the summary of reports that you reviewed when you first came on board. You wonder whether your own productivity and the productivity of your executives has improved through major changes in work approaches or whether you've just accomplished a short-term improvement by turning up the heat on every-one.

For the first time in your career, you see a clear difference between turning up the heat to improve productivity and making permanent progress through better application of talents and skills, redesigned work processes, new knowledge, and a more comprehensive sense of common purpose and unity. You recommit yourself to finding a better way to increase your own productivity in the next few years at FaraCom, and thus provide a model that will help your executives do likewise. You're pleased with the results, but you're not happy about what you've had to do to get people to become more productive at FaraCom, and you're committed to finding a better way.

This concludes your decision making at FaraCom, but you can continue playing *The Productivity Game* by choosing one of the options below.

If you want to see how your choices stack up against the other outcomes in the game, turn to Chapter 61, page 221.

If you want to discover how the other choices at your last decision-making point turned out, turn to Chapters 40 and 41, pages 155 and 157.

If you would like to embark on another decision-making track that stresses personal productivity improvements, turn to Chapter 5, Creating an Integrated Strategy and Theme, page 25.

If you'd rather begin a brand-new decision-making track that deals with building productivity in your seven division presidents, turn to Chapter 3, Increasing the Productivity of Division Presidents, page 15.

CHAPTER 43

Staying the Course

At the beginning of the year, you make a full-blown presentation to Bill Faragut regarding the progress of the three divisions that have intensified their focus on removing productivity constraints. Bill seems more or less pleased with your efforts and asks how you intend to proceed with the other divisions. You tell him that you do not plan to implement the productivity-constraint system in the other four divisions at FaraCom, a position that ignites a fierce debate.

Faragut says, "Sure. Do nothing. That way you can't possibly make a mistake."

"Hold on a minute," you shout. "Harshaw and Ferreira have already set their own productivity-improvement agendas and they're doing fine. Kofoed and Zollweg are focusing all of their time and energy on managing growth. That's exactly what they should be doing."

"Everybody in the company ought to do what these three divisions are doing."

"I disagree."

"That's obvious."

After a long silence, you remind Faragut of your philosophy, saying, "I've allowed the divisions to set their own productivity improvement agendas because I think that will bring the greatest results in the long term. I'm not ready to change that direction now."

"I don't think we've made the progress we should have."

"Bill, I've made the best judgments I can on this issue."

"That's not enough."

After another long silence, Bill Faragut stands up and says, "We're getting nowhere. Let's talk again in a few days."

As Bill Faragut leaves your office, you wonder what's really on his mind. Since you suspect he may use this issue as an excuse to remove you as CEO, you begin making a few discreet calls to let your personal network of colleagues and associates know that you may be looking for another CEOship. Thirty days later, Bill Faragut asks for your resignation and puts Sean Cope in your place. Luckily, you've laid the groundwork for a number of other job possibilities, but this marks the end of your decision making at FaraCom. Fortunately, you can continue making decisions by choosing one of the options below.

If you want to see how your choices stack up against the other outcomes in the game, turn to Chapter 61, page 221.

If you want to review the other choices you could have made at the last decision-making point, turn to Chapters 44 and 45, pages 165 and 169.

If you wish to pursue another decision-making path that emphasizes building productivity among your seven division presidents, turn to Chapter 9, Identifying the Psychological Type of Each Division President, page 41.

If you want to go onto an entirely different track that deals with building productivity in the entire organization, turn to Chapter 4, Building Productivity Throughout the Entire Organization, page 21.

CHAPTER 44

Pushing the Removal of Productivity Constraints Companywide

You reluctantly conclude that Bill Faragut will not give you the necessary time for your other four division presidents to get results with their own productivity-improvement agendas. Sensing Faragut's growing impatience with what he has called "peanuts improvements," you decide to take the bull by the horns and push the productivity-constraint-removal program companywide. In a three-day retreat with all seven division presidents, you ask Mona Sork, Alan Peay, and Sean Cope to outline their improvements over the last several months and to discuss in some detail how this approach has removed bottlenecks in every aspect of their divisions.

When the other four division presidents express uneasiness about your more forceful approach with this program, you make it clear that Bill Faragut demands more tangible productivity improvements and stronger growth in revenues and profits.

You conclude, "Time has run out, folks. We've got to make major strides in our productivity companywide, and we've got to do it in the next few months."

David Zollweg shakes his head. "Why didn't you tell us this a year ago?"

Startled by the question, you answer, somewhat sheepishly, "I was trying to give you free reign over your divisions, but that hasn't worked in every case."

"I can't speak for everyone," remarks Zollweg, "but I didn't know that Bill Faragut was so displeased about our progress."

"I accept responsibility for that. I have probably insulated you too much from his demands and expectations."

"You're the boss."

It seems you're getting your point across when everyone becomes more serious about implementing the productivity constraint system. Carefully using the experience and enthusiasm of Sork, Peay, and Cope, you help the other four division presidents develop plans and schedules for initiating their first attacks on bottlenecks in their divisions. Within a few months, everyone has made measurable progress in enhancing productivity, and at a management meeting Lisa Harshaw sums up the general feeling by saying, "I wish we'd started this three years ago. We have been able to cut three months out of our old nine-month book production schedule and it's made a big difference in our ability to acquire manuscripts and get them to the market quickly."

By year end, sales grow to $880 million, with profits climbing to $60 million, as shown below:

Selected Financial and Productivity Information
(Revenues and Profits in $ Millions)

	Fifth Year	*Fourth Year*
Revenues	$880	$749
Profits	60	20
Employees	2,258	1,980
Revenues per Employee (Actual $)	$389,725	$378,283
Profits per Employee (Actual $)	$26,572	$10,101

Progress during this last year satisfies Bill Faragut sufficiently that he compliments you on your work. In retrospect, as you look back over your five years of decision making at FaraCom, one stark reality stands out: You moved too slowly. FaraCom's divisions could have accomplished much more had you given them more decisive direction from the top.

This marks the end of this decision-making track, but you can continue playing the game by pursuing one of the following options.

If you want to find out how your decision making on this path ranks with other possibilities in The Productivity Game, *turn to Chapter 61, page 221.*

To review the other choices you could have made at the last decision-making point, turn to Chapters 43 and 45, pages 163 and 169.

If you would like to pursue another decision-making track that deals with building the productivity of your seven division presidents, turn to Chapter 9, Identifying the Psychological Type of Each Division President, page 41.

To embark upon a totally different decision-making path that builds the productivity of the entire organization, turn to Chapter 4, Building Productivity Throughout the Entire Organization, page 21.

CHAPTER 45

Turning Your Attention to External Acquisitions

You immediately look outside FaraCom for a major acquisition you can accomplish quickly. That, you assume, will add sufficient growth to take the pressure off overall performance during the coming year. You're convinced that Bill Faragut won't let up and that the only way you can satisfy him will be to add a healthy new company to the FaraCom family.

As you investigate acquisition candidates, the word spreads quickly throughout the organization that your panic has forced you to try to pull a rabbit out of a hat. When the rumors reach Bill Faragut, it marks the beginning of the end for your tenure as CEO.

Over the next few weeks, Bill Faragut scrutinizes your activities, asking your division presidents and other employees at corporate headquarters for their reactions. He concludes that your shift in focus has revealed a major weakness in your managerial capabilities. "You're panicking or trying to cover up your lack of progress," says Faragut as he confronts you in your office.

"We're simply trying to bring another dimension of growth to the company."

"I don't buy it. Why not keep your focus on existing operations? They need to become more productive."

"I agree, but a new acquisition will not only benefit the company, it will give the other divisions time to implement their productivity improvements."

Bill Faragut grunts as he leaves your office.

Before long, you hear rumors of Bill Faragut's search for a CEO to replace you. Seeing the handwriting on the wall, you decide to leave FaraCom before you're terminated, and you accept a position as a principal of a small but prestigious management consulting firm.

This marks the end of your decision making at FaraCom, but you can continue playing *The Productivity Game* by choosing one of the options below.

To see how this outcome compares to other possibilities, turn to Chapter 61, page 221.

If you want to consider the other choices you could have made in your last decision, turn to Chapters 43 and 44, pages 163 and 165.

If you would like to pursue another decision-making track that deals with improving the productivity of your seven division presidents, turn to Chapter 9, Identifying the Psychological Type of Each Division President, page 41.

If you would rather embark on an entirely different productivity decision-making path that focuses on total company productivity, turn to Chapter 4, Building Productivity Throughout the Entire Organization, page 21.

CHAPTER 46

Pursuing an Aggressive Implementation of the Three-Step Cycle

Convinced that your three-step cycle represents a major advance in management thought and practice, you see no reason not to permeate it throughout FaraCom's operations as quickly as possible. Like a zealot, you preach your three-step doctrine in every interchange with executives, managers, and employees throughout the company. Employees begin to call you "the preacher" and refer to your three-step doctrine as a new "religion."

At first you don't see the down side of the comparisons, but within a few months you encounter a backlash of strong frustrations and resentments. Employees claim your system prevents people from growing, expanding, and changing. They also cite numerous misjudgments and misinterpretations of their behavior and attitudes, accusing you of fostering a system that discriminates against so-called doers, while providing an elite status for knowers and be-ers. In one case, a group of four disgruntled "doing" oriented middle managers were told by Janice Kofoed that research suggests there is an abundance of doers in the general population and a scarcity of knowers and be-ers. "Consequently," she said, "if you're a knower or a be-er, you stand a better chance of getting promoted."

When a dozen people threaten lawsuits, every FaraCom division falls into an abyss of chaos. As hard as you try, you cannot turn the tide of pent-up resentment evident throughout the organization. You're surprised at how quickly the morale and mood of the company has plunged in just a few months.

Having learned a hard and difficult lesson, you decide you should remove yourself as CEO, turning the reins over to Sean Cope, one of the voices most critical of your aggressive all-out implementation of the three-step cycle. Bill Faragut accepts your decision, but regrets losing you and asks you to remain on as a member of the board of directors. You agree, but decide to devote most of your attention to writing a book about your three-step cycle and establishing a small consulting practice to help companies implement the program appropriately. A few months later, Sean Cope tells you that your three-step cycle continues to provide benefits to the company, but he confides, "We're not trying to force it on anyone."

This marks the end of your decision making at FaraCom, but you can continue playing *The Productivity Game* by selecting one of the options below.

If you want to see how this outcome compares to other possibilities, turn to Chapter 61, page 221.

If you want to examine the other two choices you could have made at the last decision-making point, turn to Chapters 47 and 48, pages 173 and 175.

To pursue another decision-making path that also relates to building the productivity of your seven division presidents, turn to Chapter 10, Hiring an Outside Consultant, page 49.

If you would like to embark on a totally different decision-making path that deals with building productivity throughout the entire organization, turn to Chapter 4, Building Productivity Throughout the Entire Organization, page 21.

CHAPTER 47

Using a Balanced and Tempered Approach to Implement the Three-Step Cycle

Considering the other two extremes too aggressive or overly cautious, and perhaps deadly to the success of your three-step cycle, you begin laying the groundwork with your seven division presidents to ensure that people do not abuse the three steps in any FaraCom operation or function. You stress that the knowing, being, doing steps represent only guidelines for action and decision making, rather than a hard and fast formula for compensation, promotion, or employee evaluation. You bring in experts from Hill & Knowlton, a large public relations and communications firm, to document and communicate the three-step cycle in language that won't offend or prejudice anyone in the organization.

After a full six months of preparation, you launch your three-step cycle first with your division presidents and their management teams as a guideline for making strategic business decisions and executive selection choices. In a meeting with your seven division presidents you make it clear: "For the next two years, I want to temper use of the three-step cycle so that we avoid abuses and yet gain the maximum benefit from what I think all of us consider an enlightened way of managing an enterprise."

Responding to your advice, Sean Cope, head of catalog sales and direct marketing, comments, "There's no question this kind of approach invites abuse. I think you're wise to stress balance and temperance. For me, as a doer, I worry that knowers and be-ers will become a favored or elite corps within the company, bringing about a devaluation of the doing function, which could really hurt the company."

Your other seven division presidents agree to commit themselves to a balanced and tempered implementation for a two-year period, during which time they will use the guidelines of the three-step cycle within their management teams but limit its use outside that level.

As the months unfold, productivity at FaraCom increases as your seven division presidents continue to shift assignments and carefully identify company situations, market conditions, and the application of executive talent by cautiously using the three-step cycle for the benefit of every FaraCom division. By year end, sales jump to $1.4 billion, with profits reaching $200 million, as shown below:

Selected Financial and Productivity Information
(Revenues and Profits in $ Millions)

	Fifth Year	Fourth Year
Revenues	$1,404	$1,038
Profits	201	104
Employees	2,694	2,064
Revenues per Employee (Actual $)	$521,158	$502,907
Profits per Employee (Actual $)	$74,610	$50,388

Looking back over your five years as CEO of FaraCom, you realize that the most powerful ideas and concepts lend themselves to abuse if applied too harshly. In some cases, caution makes a lot of sense.

This marks the end of this decision-making track, but you can continue playing *The Productivity Game* by pursuing one of the options below.

If you would like to see how this decision-making track stacks up against other outcomes in the game, turn to Chapter 61, page 221.

To discover what results the other choices available to you at your last decision-making point produced, turn to Chapters 46 and 48, pages 171 and 175.

If you wish to pursue a different decision-making path that deals with building productivity among your seven division presidents, turn to Chapter 10, Hiring an Outside Consultant, page 49.

If you want to embark on an entirely different decision-making path, turn to Chapter 4, Building Productivity Throughout the Entire Organization page 21.

CHAPTER 48

Taking a Cautious, Limited Approach to Implementing the Three-Step Cycle

Recognizing that the three-step cycle can invite abuse, you decide to proceed with an extremely cautious and limited implementation of the approach. The previous two-step cycle matches the age-old "strategy formulation/strategy implementation" cycle and does not seem to threaten people with different capabilities. However, the three-step cycle introduces a greater differentiation among people and their preferences, which could cause discrimination and a potentially damaging corporate class system. With this in mind, you choose to apply the three-step cycle with your seven division presidents only as a rough guideline, rather than as a firm operating philosophy, and certainly not as a corporate policy. You promote discussion of the approach in meetings with your seven division presidents, but at every junction you warn them against relying upon it too heavily.

Slowly but surely the seven division presidents begin to use the three-step cycle guideline to shift assignments and meet customer needs. For example, David Zollweg, president of software and CD-ROM publishing, uses the three-step cycle to better categorize and manage the product life cycle stages of different product lines. He reports, "Mature product lines need doers, growing product lines need be-ers, and start-up product lines need knowers." However, taking heed of your own cautiousness, Zollweg and the other division presidents avoid overuse of the concept and minimize its discussion in their divisions.

While you don't make the progress you had hoped for by the end of your fifth year as CEO of FaraCom, you firmly believe that an abuse of the three-step system could have done more harm than good. By year end, sales growth has stagnated, reaching only $1.15 billion, with profits of $120 million, as shown below:

Selected Financial and Productivity Information
(Revenues and Profits in $ Millions)

	Fifth Year	*Fourth Year*
Revenues	$1,152	$1,038
Profits	120	104
Employees	2,288	2,064
Revenues per Employee (Actual $)	$503,497	$502,907
Profits per Employee (Actual $)	$52,448	$50,388

In retrospect, after discussing the matter at length with your seven division presidents, you conclude that your cautiousness has proven somewhat extreme. You concur that a wider, slightly more aggressive application of the three-step system will produce greater improvements in productivity in the future. Having erred on the side of caution, you're grateful that your career remains intact, but you know you must step up implementation of the three-step cycle in the coming year.

This marks the end of your decision-making path; however, you can continue playing *The Productivity Game* by selecting one of the options below.

If you would like to see how this decision-making track stacks up against the outcomes of others, turn to Chapter 61, page 221.

If you want to review the other two choices you could have made at your last decision-making point, turn to Chapters 46 and 47, pages 171 and 173.

If you choose to pursue another decision-making track that relates to building the productivity of your seven division presidents, turn to Chapter 10, Hiring an Outside Consultant, page 49.

To embark upon a totally different decision-making track that builds productivity throughout FaraCom, turn to Chapter 4, Building Productivity Throughout the Entire Organization, page 21.

CHAPTER 49

Executing a Formal Companywide Roll-Out of the Three Fields of Work

You finally convince yourself that the time has come to shift your attention away from the seven division presidents' productivity to that of the entire organization. Since FaraCom has never reached productivity levels as high as those experienced in the last year, you believe that rolling out the concept of working in three different fields on a daily, weekly, monthly, and yearly basis will do more than anything else to transform the company at every level of the organization.

You spend the next month assembling a team of inside and outside experts, human resource specialists, instructional designers, presenters, and facilitators to develop this companywide launch. You want everything to be perfect in terms of communicating concepts, providing examples, facilitating training, and executing implementation. You'll have only one opportunity to get the companywide roll-out right.

Your excitement builds as you get closer to May 1, the target date for the companywide roll-out. You sense some concern among your seven division presidents that this focus on working in the three fields could distract the attention of FaraCom employees to the point that it takes their eyes off customers and the work at hand. At one point, a four-hour debate erupts among your division presidents over whether everyone in the organization or just management should apply the three fields of work.

Mona Sork, president of retail operations, represents one side, "We shouldn't burden our employees with a lot of philosophy about fields of

177

work. The concepts benefit senior managers because they have to worry about that sort of thing anyway, but it could become a distraction to employees in general. This is a classic 'need to know' issue, and I don't think everybody needs to know this stuff."

Lisa Harshaw, president of book publishing, represents the other side, "We can't afford not sharing this with every employee. It's a major breakthrough in thinking about work. It's made each of us much more productive. Everyone in the company can benefit from understanding and applying the three fields of work."

You finally quell the debate by insisting, "By definition, the three fields of work will help any individual better perform his or her assigned tasks, duties, and responsibilities." You make it clear that you will not tolerate additional debate on this issue and expect every division president to support the roll-out actively and fully.

Over the next few months your worst nightmare becomes a reality as the prophecy of some of your seven division presidents proves true. Mona Sork, president of retail operations, quickly reminds you, "We tried to warn you."

Employees become so enthralled discussing, interpreting, and applying the three fields of work that sales drop at year end to $1.1 billion, and profits decline to $92 million, as shown below:

Selected Financial and Productivity Information
(Revenues and Profits in $ Millions)

	Fifth Year	Fourth Year
Revenues	$1,096	$1,221
Profits	92	123
Employees	2,448	2,451
Revenues per Employee (Actual $)	$447,712	$498,164
Profits per Employee (Actual $)	$37,582	$50,184

Retrospectively, you feel good about your five years as CEO of FaraCom, but this last year's stagnation concerns you and Bill Faragut. Since you're still not willing to concede that the three fields of work cannot produce spectacular results, you commit to finding a better way for spreading this concept and its application throughout the entire organization.

This marks the end of your decision making on this track, but you can continue to play *The Productivity Game* by choosing one of the options below.

If you would like to see how this decision-making track stacks up against the other outcomes, turn to Chapter 61, page 221.

To see how the other two choices from your last decision-making point turned out, turn to Chapters 50 and 51, pages 181 and 185.

If you want to pursue another decision-making track that deals with building the productivity of your seven division presidents, turn to Chapter 8, Allowing the Seven Division Presidents to Set Their Own Agendas, page 37.

To embark on a totally different decision-making track that focuses on companywide productivity, turn to Chapter 4, Building Productivity Throughout the Entire Organization, page 21.

CHAPTER 50

Spreading the Word Informally

In the world of ideas you believe that the best ones always get passed along vigorously, without threat, without offense. In light of this belief, you conclude that informally spreading the word regarding the three fields of work throughout the FaraCom organization beats all other approaches because it's natural and free. You ask each of your division presidents to share with their people what's taken place in their own lives, how the concepts of working in three different fields have affected their performance. "But," you emphasize, "do not demand that anyone else adopt the framework."

In what your division presidents call an eloquent speech, you characterize your feelings at a one-day management retreat with FaraCom's top 100 executives: "Many of you have asked about my commitment to this new framework we call the three fields of work. It works for me. It's had a phenomenal impact on my own personal productivity, and I no longer take any action or make any decision without considering which field of work I'm occupying at the time. Each of the division presidents has also gained insights with the concept. It's not a company program or policy, but if you'd like to know more about it, we'd be happy to share more of our experiences with you."

Sure enough, in the months that follow, employees throughout the FaraCom organization find out more and more about the three fields of work and you, along with your seven division presidents, enjoy talking about your own transformations.

In a private meeting you have with Alan Peay, president of magazine publishing, he expresses a common viewpoint, "When an idea's right, people pay attention. And when an idea works, people adopt it. That's happening all over FaraCom. I'm glad we didn't try to stuff this down their throats. It wouldn't have worked."

Not surprisingly, you receive hundreds of letters from employees throughout the company expressing their appreciation for a work environment that encourages work in all three fields and helps them achieve a better personal and professional balance. The letters started flowing in about three months ago, after you encouraged feedback through your division presidents and through company communications as a way of giving people the opportunity to share their stories of productivity improvement. Now, almost half of FaraCom's monthly newsletter contains testimonials about productivity improvements. One testimonial from a cinematographer in the film- and video-production division expressed deep appreciation: "I'm naturally inclined toward the 'completing work' field, and I think I'm pretty good at what I do, but my peers and associates often think I'm a pain to work with. I've never tried to do much about how I often offend and antagonize others until now. The three fields of work helped me realize for the first time that there is an important and necessary field of work called 'unifying work' that pulls people together in a common cause. Strangely, I'd never thought about it like that before. Now, I try to do some 'unifying work' every day. I think my associates will agree that we've all become more productive in the process."

In another testimonial, a software engineer in the software and CD-ROM publishing division admits: "I live for the opportunity to discover breakthroughs. 'Magnifying work' is the field of work I love because it lets me create new products. However, the three fields of work have helped me realize I need to spend more time debugging new products and refining existing versions. 'Completing work' keeps the division profitable day in and day out. Sometimes I forget that identifying the work that needs to get done today is also vitally important."

At year end, sales increase to $1.3 billion and profits climb to $150 million, as shown by the following:

Selected Financial and Productivity Information
(Revenues and Profits in $ Millions)

	Fifth Year	*Fourth Year*
Revenues	$1,315	$1,221
Profits	149	123
Employees	2,563	2,451
Revenues per Employee (Actual $)	$513,070	$498,164
Profits per Employee (Actual $)	$58,135	$50,184

Retrospectively, you acknowledge that the new thinking about work has provided a kernel of truth that has fueled a true productivity transformation at FaraCom. As you look forward to next year, you adopt, as FaraCom's theme for the future, a phrase from an article written about FaraCom in *Business Week:* "They build productivity one person at a time."

This marks the end of your decision making on this track, but you can continue playing *The Productivity Game* by selecting one of the options below.

If you want to find out how this decision-making track stacks up against the outcomes of others, turn to Chapter 61, page 221.

To discover what happened to the other two choices you could have made at your last decision-making point, turn to Chapters 49 and 51, pages 177 and 185.

If you would like to pursue another decision-making track that deals with improving the productivity of your seven division presidents, turn to Chapter 8, Allowing the Seven Division Presidents to Set Their Own Agendas, page 37.

To embark upon an entirely different decision-making path that addresses companywide productivity from the beginning, turn to Chapter 4, Building Productivity Throughout the Entire Organization, page 21.

CHAPTER 51

Keeping Your Focus on the Seven Division Presidents

Overcoming the temptation to spread the word about the three fields of work formally or informally throughout the organization, you decide to return to your original focus: building the productivity of your seven division presidents. Since you believe the fallout from their productivity gains will certainly influence the organization in innumerable ways over the next few years, you immediately begin talking with the compensation committee of the board of directors to create the appropriate golden handcuffs that will keep your seven division presidents on board, passing along to others their experiences with heightened productivity.

In addition to improving the compensation of your senior executives, you spend the coming year discussing with them the implications of working in the three fields and how doing so affects operations in each division. You plan monthly full-day sessions in which the division presidents can share their experiences relating to the three fields of work. You believe that keeping them learning and growing in all three fields will maximize overall productivity at FaraCom in the long term. Knowing that different people naturally function better in one field or the other, with few able to do so in all of them, you think the sharing of experiences will strengthen the development of holistic, balanced, broad-gauged, as well as focused executives.

As the months unfold, you stress one field of work each month, bringing in experts to speak at lunch, as well as facilitators, to expand upon the understanding, knowledge, and awareness regarding the many facets of work in a particular field. One month you bring in Edward de Bono, a leading authority on thinking and the author of several books including *Six Thinking Hats*, to talk about "magnifying work." Another month you ask Harvard Business School Professor Len Schlesinger, author of *The Real Heroes of Business and Not a CEO Among Them*, to speak on "unifying work." On another occasion you invite Andrew Grove, president of Intel and author of *High Output Management* to address the subject of "completing work."

After a few months of listening to professors, authors, consultants, and other experts talk about the new world of work, you decide to include more outstanding achievers like Andrew Grove in each field of work to speak to your senior team, hoping these role models will teach by example. You invite Bill Gates, CEO of Microsoft, to talk about "magnifying work," Max DePree, former CEO of Herman Miller, to address "unifying work," and Eckhard Pfeiffer, CEO of Compaq Computer, to speak on "completing work." In addition to the monthly one-day sessions, you schedule a full day each month with each one of your division presidents to review operations in an off-site, probing discussion of productivity in each of the three fields of work.

As the year unfolds, your concentration on building and improving the productivity of your seven division presidents, combined with an enhanced compensation package with stock options and a smorgasbord of bonuses, fuels a genuine transformation at FaraCom.

In one day-long retreat with your seven presidents, Sean Cope, president of cable television operations, reports that greater emphasis on "magnifying work" has produced three new television programming thrusts in historical profiles, gourmet growing, and home officing. Mona Sork, president of retail operations, reveals that more emphasis on "unifying work" has created several new buying-merchandising teams that run circles around the old organizational approach. Alan Peay, president of magazine publishing, points to their newly implemented process of breaking work down into the three fields as the major contributor to recent productivity gains. David Zollweg, president of software and CD-ROM publishing, cites the blending of all three fields of work on a daily basis for his division's recent 25 percent increase in sales and profits. Janice Kofoed, president of catalog sales and direct marketing, reports that more emphasis on "completing work" removed major bottlenecks and facilitated a reengineering of the entire soliciting, order-taking, servicing, and fulfillment work flow. Stephen Ferreira, president of film and video production, tells how people in his division use the language of the three fields of work to communicate with one another about what work needs to occur, "We've never been more productive," he says. Lisa Harshaw, president of book publishing, tells how her division's spring list of books has doubled because her employees have learned to do more "magnifying work" and in the process reinvented book publishing.

Without officially spreading the word about the three fields of work throughout the company, the seven division presidents themselves become role models for people at all lower levels, increasing the amount of personal discussion, coaching, and mentoring about productivity and performance. As a result, so many people surpass past peak performances that sales to climb to $1.5 billion for the year, with profits of $180 million, as shown below:

Selected Financial and Productivity Information
(Revenues and Profits in $ Millions)

	Fifth Year	*Fourth Year*
Revenues	$1,521	$1,221
Profits	181	123
Employees	2,936	2,451
Revenues per Employee (Actual $)	$518,052	$498,164
Profits per Employee (Actual $)	$61,649	$50,184

As you look back on your five years as CEO of FaraCom, you take pride in the fact that your focus on building the productivity of your seven division presidents via the three fields of work has effectively deployed their talents in each of their businesses.

In January of your sixth year as CEO, Bill Faragut decides to step down as chairman of the board and makes you chairman and CEO, announcing that FaraCom will go public sometime during the year and promising you 15 percent stock ownership. *Forbes* magazine picks up on the productivity improvement at FaraCom and your unusual personalized approach to building productivity in your key executives. A cover story at the end of January heralds you as "a New Age productivity builder."

This marks the end of your decision making on this decision track, but you can continue playing *The Productivity Game* by selecting one of the following options.

If you want to see how this outcome ranks among other outcomes, turn to Chapter 61, page 221.

To review the choices you could have made at your last decision-making point, turn to Chapters 49 and 50, pages 177 and 181.

If you wish to pursue another decision making track that focuses on building productivity in your seven division presidents, turn to Chapter 8, Allowing the Seven Division Presidents to Set Their Own Agendas, page 37.

To embark on a totally different track, that focuses on building productivity companywide, turn to Chapter 4, Building Productivity Throughout the Entire Organization, page 21.

CHAPTER 52

Adopting an Employee Productivity Program

After a quick but thorough search of the recent literature on productivity, you decide to explore Robert Sibson's 12-step EP (employee productivity) process, which seems to embody all the latest thinking on the subject. You begin by implementing Sibson's first four steps:

1. Getting executive commitment—making sure senior management is committed to productivity management.
2. Developing a productivity culture—building productivity consciousness throughout the organization.
3. Making productivity part of every manager's job—assigning the job of productivity management to every manager.
4. Measuring productivity—establishing productivity measures for every organizational unit throughout the company.

As you launch your emphasis on these four steps through management meetings, retreats, performance reviews, and a variety of other communications throughout each of the company's divisions, you find yourself wondering how much time Bill Faragut will let pass before he intervenes. Sean Cope, president of cable television operations, reminds you that Faragut wants results immediately, "Are you sure Faragut will give us the time we need to implement this program? He seems quite anxious for immediate improvements."

"I know, but he's got to give us time to make this program work."

"I hope you're right."

As each division deals with these first four steps, you encourage your senior team to move quickly to the second stage of productivity improvement by embracing Sibson's next eight steps, which include:

1. Using technology more effectively—understanding new technology and the proper utilization of machines.

2. Eliminating unproductive practices—launching a vendetta against unproductive practices of any type everywhere in the organization.

3. Empowering employees—delegating responsibility for productivity improvement to the lowest levels.

4. Utilizing networking—giving every worker access to information and experience that will be helpful in achieving work excellence.

5. Ensuring excellence in staffing—recruiting effective people and giving them the correct assignments.

6. Restructuring through streamlining and possible staff reduction—eliminating one or more organizational levels.

7. Managing performance—establishing performance appraisal and training as key parts of performance management.

8. Rewarding performance—giving people the incentive to increase the effectiveness of their work.

Within a few months these 12 concepts begin to take hold within the organization as the divisions eliminate organizational layers, establish measures, emphasize training, and increase productivity consciousness throughout the company. You can, however, supply only anecdotal evidence to support that fact because sales and profits per employee show little change. While you collect many success stories from around the company to share with Bill Faragut, you sense he has already adopted another agenda. He seems almost indifferent to your presentation.

Two weeks later you discover that Bill Faragut has for several weeks been searching for a CEO to replace you. When he informs you of your termination, he offers an attractive severance package, saying, "We appreciate your contribution to FaraCom, but I feel it's time to move forward under new leadership."

This marks the end of your decision making at FaraCom, but you can continue playing *The Productivity Game* by selecting one of the options below.

If you want to see how this outcome compares to other possibilities, turn to Chapter 61, page 221.

If you want to consider the other two choices from the last decision-making point, turn to Chapters 53 and 54, pages 193 and 197.

If you want to pursue another decision-making path that deals with building productivity throughout the entire organization, turn to Chapter 12, Implementing Covey's "First Things First" Philosophy, page 57.

If you would like to embark on a totally different decision-making track that stresses building your own productivity, turn to Chapter 2, Maximizing Your Own Productivity, page 11.

CHAPTER 53

Sending Executives to an Off-Site Productivity-Improvement Program

After searching diligently for the right kind of program to build productivity among the top 74 managers at FaraCom, you settle on John Scherer's Executive Development Intensive (EDI). Scherer's intensive one-on-one program does not come out of an abstract theory or a marketing scheme to push his productivity workshops, but rather from a genuine response to the real needs of executives aimed at helping them find themselves and in the process develop greater effectiveness in their work.

The EDI program addresses the whole person in an integrated way, one executive at a time. Only the executive and his or her spouse work with the EDI staff to ensure privacy and the kind of deep questioning and probing necessary to build productivity permanently and help executives put life back into their work. When Stephen Ferreira, president of film and video production, and his wife, Andrea, go through the program, they begin with a written questionnaire that comes a few weeks before the week-long intensive. The questionnaire covers descriptions of important relationships, their physical health, eating habits, issues of concern on the job, and objectives for the intensive. After arriving for the week-long intensive, Stephen and Andrea begin each day with a personal exercise coach and 45 minutes of walking, jogging, aerobics, biking, swimming, or weight training.

Next, they do yoga with their own yoga instructor for 45 minutes, followed by a shower and breakfast. At 9 o'clock facilitators begin one-on-one sessions that take Stephen and Andrea through a kind of personal archaeology that examines decisions they've made about how to exist in the world. Stephen Ferreira finds out that the "self" he has portrayed to the world is a facade that hides a fear of being engaged in meaningless work. The facilitator tells Ferreira that "facades, the ways we deal with threats and dangers, represent personal success formulas that are nothing more than con games we consider necessary for happiness and prosperity." The one-on-one session continues throughout the morning in an effort to help Ferreira evaluate whether his "con" or "facade" is worthy of his energies and attention. Following lunch, body work begins, based on the following assumptions: "(1) Body, mind, and spirit are a continuum, (2) The body is one of the most direct avenues to the human spirit, and (3) The body is a metaphor for the con game that the mind, left to its own devices, usually plays on the world." Through specialized stretching, yoga therapy, and deep muscle massage, Stephen and Andrea work to transcend the limitations of the mind. The next three days repeat the first with some variations such as imaginary conversations with living or dead significant others in their lives and new purpose explorations. On the final day, Stephen and Andrea create a plan of action designed to transform their old selves into something with greater possibility. Over the next three months three in-depth telephone reviews with their facilitators occur.

After your first four executives (Ferreira, Harshaw, Kofoed, and Peay) return from their week-long experiences, you imagine just how valuable the EDI will prove over the next few years as all executives and managers gain similar insights from the program. You yourself went through EDI, learning firsthand that "if work injures the human spirit, even if it's profitable, it proves fatal in the end because it destroys the human spirit."

You and the other four executives who have attended over the last six weeks have identified quite clearly the slow suffocation of life in the executive suite when work and the human spirit do not go hand in hand. EDI's emphasis on the whole person and putting the human spirit back into work has changed your life and your outlook. The other four executives feel similarly. Unfortunately, when Bill Faragut investigates EDI on his own, he refers to it as "warm and fuzzy nonsense" and publicly reprimands you for going off on such an unproductive tangent.

A local AP writer catches wind of the brewing conflict at FaraCom and writes a two-page article in which he quotes Bill Faragut as saying, "Our company is in business to serve its customers and make a profit. We're not in the business of helping people find themselves. That's a job for the shrinks."

When the gap between you and Bill Faragut widens, you decide to tender your resignation six months before the end of your fifth year as CEO. On the bright side, however, your experience with EDI has so altered your perspective about work and the human spirit that it puts you into a totally new kind of job search mode. You're confident you'll now be able to find the right environment in which to work. One opportunity that looks particularly intriguing is the offer to become an EDI facilitator.

This marks the end of your decision making on this track, but you can continue playing *The Productivity Game* by selecting one of the options below.

If you would like to compare this outcome to other possibilities, turn to Chapter 61, page 221.

If you want to find out how the other choices at your last decision-making point turned out, turn to Chapters 52 and 54, pages 189 and 197.

To pursue another decision-making track that deals with building productivity throughout the organization, turn to Chapter 12, Implementing Covey's "First Things First" Philosophy, page 57.

If you would like to embark on a totally different decision-making track that focuses on building your own productivity, turn to Chapter 2, Maximizing Your Own Productivity, page 11.

CHAPTER 54

Reorganizing to Create an Environment That Promotes Productivity

To build a new environment at FaraCom that will promote greater productivity improvements, you draw on the work of Marvin Weisbord, author of *Productive Work Places*. Specifically, you use Weisbord's summary of the work of three organizational behaviorists (Kurt Lewin, Eric Trist, and Fred Emery) to describe the necessary environment for making work satisfying. According to Weisbord, satisfying work involves six intrinsic factors:

1. Variety and challenge—plenty of opportunity.
2. Elbow room for decision making—more flexibility than rigidity.
3. Feedback and learning—a lot of coaching and mentoring.
4. Mutual support and respect—genuine care and concern.
5. Wholeness and meaning—purposeful work abounds.
6. Room to grow—a bright future.

You know you must balance the first three factors: "Not too much, which adds stress and anxiety, nor too little, which produces stultifying tedium." The second group of three factors are open ended, "no one can have too much respect, growing room, or wholeness—meaning a view of both the origin and the customer's use of your work." Using these six intrinsic factors, you charge your seven division presidents with the task and challenge of creating work environments that make sure that these six intrinsic factors of satisfying work get maximized.

When Bill Faragut learns about what you're doing, he calls it "too academic" and applies more pressure on you to build real productivity and tangible results. However, you remain convinced that paying attention to the six factors of satisfying work will build productivity throughout the organization once your division presidents and their management teams make the necessary reorganizations and "mind-set" changes. You decide to ignore Bill Faragut and his skepticism by moving forward full steam with your plan to make FaraCom a productive work place.

With the help of Marvin Weisbord's consulting firm, Block-Petrella-Weisbord, you work hard over the next few months to make sure that the six factors remain vibrant throughout FaraCom's culture. Consultants from Block-Petrella-Weisbord use a helpful visual to help executives and managers make the necessary changes:

Old Paradigm *(Early 20th Century)*	*New Paradigm* *(Late 20th Century)*
• Technology first	• Social/technical systems optimized together
• People as machine extension	• People complement machine
• People as spare parts	• People as scarce resources
• Narrow tasks, simple skills	• Multiple, broad skills
• External control: procedures	• Self-control: teams
• Many levels, autocratic style	• Flat organization, participative style
• Competitive	• Cooperative
• Organization's purposes only	• Individual and social purposes included
• Alienation: "It's only a job"	• Commitment: "It's my job"
• Low risk taking	• Innovation

The consultants argue "Only informed self-control, not close supervision, will work in the new economy. The new paradigm of the late twentieth century is quickly revolutionizing organizations throughout the world."

The foregoing chart helps people in every division come to realize FaraCom's commitment to creating a new kind of work place, one that meets the needs of the late twentieth century, especially the needs of employees striving to become more productive.

By year end, sales reach $950 million, with profits climbing to $88 million, as shown below:

Selected Financial and Productivity Information
(Revenues and Profits in $ Millions)

	Fifth Year	Fourth Year
Revenues	$949	$802
Profits	88	18
Employees	2,396	2,001
Revenues per Employee (Actual $)	$396,077	$400,799
Profits per Employee (Actual $)	$36,728	$8,996

Though these numbers force Bill Faragut to back off a bit, he still seems unconvinced that you know what you're doing. He's still living in the old paradigm. Fortunately, you feel good about your decision making and believe that FaraCom will continue to make progress in results and productivity by paying continuous attention to the factors that create satisfying work in a productive work place. Your division presidents feel similarly. David Zollweg sums it up nicely in your annual management retreat after the first of the year, "We have created an environment where every employee can grow, develop, and contribute. Last year we saw more emphasis on teams, more focus on performance challenges for teams and individuals, more flexible operating processes, more individualized development through coaching, more attention paid to blending personal and professional goals, and fewer restrictions on growth, advancement, and change. I'm proud to be here."

This marks the end of your decision making on this track, but you can continue to play *The Productivity Game* by choosing one of the options that follow.

If you would like to see how this decision-making track stacks up against the other outcomes, turn to Chapter 61, page 221.

If you want to review the choices you could have made at your last decision-making point, turn to Chapters 52 and 53, pages 189 and 193.

If you would like to pursue another decision-making track that deals with building the productivity of the entire organization, turn to Chapter 12, Implementing Covey's "First Things First" Philosophy, page 57.

To embark on a totally different decision-making track that focuses on your own productivity, turn to Chapter 2, Maximizing Your Own Productivity, page 11.

CHAPTER 55

Teaching People to Make Principle-Centered Choices

According to the Covey Leadership Organization, every moment of choice represents a moment of truth, a testing point of character and competence that shapes an organization after all the collective choices come together. Making choices based on principles, or what you refer to as "principle-centered choice," means always considering the principle at stake or the principle involved in every moment that requires a choice. To help employees of FaraCom implement this idea of principle-centered choices, you use Covey's three-step process:

1. Ask with intent: Ask your conscience, not out of curiosity, but out of commitment, to act based on the wisdom of the heart.

    What's the best use of my time right now?

    What's the most important right now?

    What is life asking of me?

    What's the right thing to do now?

    Is this in my circle of influence?

    Is it in my center of focus?

    Is there a third alternative solution?

    What principles apply?

    What is the best way to apply them?

2. Listen without excuse: "When we hear the first whispering of conscience, we do one of two things—we either act in harmony with it, or we immediately begin to rationalize—tell ourselves 'rational lies'—as to why we should make some other choice."

3. Act with courage: "Some of the greatest acts of courage are in that instant between stimulus and response in our everyday decisions in life."

To help all employees learn how to make principle-centered choices, you engage the Covey Leadership Organization to conduct workshops throughout the organization and to instruct in-house trainers to carry it to lower levels so that everyone learns how to implement these three steps to improved decision making. Throughout the FaraCom organization, whenever major team, department, or division decisions are made, the three-step process is employed. According to one team leader in the catalog sales and direct marketing division, "We faced a tough dilemma: how to spend more time communicating with customers to ensure their satisfaction while at the same time increasing the number of telephone calls handled per hour. After asking the three principle-centered questions, we decided to follow our conscience by worrying more about satisfying customers and less about increasing the number of calls handled. We made the right decision because the increased sales per customer greatly outweighed the impact of the decreased number of calls per hour."

As the year unfolds, you receive feedback from your division presidents that this focus on principle-centered choice has made a big difference in their divisions as people everywhere at all levels take more time to think about their choices, to pay attention to their consciences, and to worry about the underlying principles of the organization. Even one of your toughest-minded and deepest-thinking executives, David Zollweg, president of software and CD-ROM publishing, praises the program: "My people are actually learning how to see principles in changing circumstances. They used to be driven by circumstance and situation, but now they're learning to rise above that and live by principles. It's cut bad and poor decision making in half, and we're still improving."

At year end, sales reach $1.3 billion with profits climbing to $168 million, as shown by the following:

Selected Financial and Productivity Information
(Revenues and Profits in $ Millions)

	Fifth Year	Fourth Year
Revenues	$1,308	$1,009
Profits	168	131
Employees	2,515	1,943
Revenues per Employee (Actual $)	$520,080	$519,300
Profits per Employee (Actual $)	$66,799	$67,422

The Covey Leadership Organization uses FaraCom as a prime example of a principle-centered company and touts your leadership in their seminars and workshops throughout the world, bringing new attention and praise to the company. In retrospect, you believe you have taken FaraCom to a new level of performance that will bring even greater results in the future.

This marks the end of your decision making on this track, but you can continue playing *The Productivity Game* by selecting one of the options below.

If you would like to see how this outcome ranks with other outcomes in the game, turn to Chapter 61, page 221.

If you want to review the choices you could have made at your last decision-making point, turn to Chapters 56 and 57, pages 205 and 209.

To pursue another decision-making track that also deals with building productivity throughout the entire organization, turn to Chapter 13, Installing EmpowerTech's Improvement System, page 61.

To embark on a totally different decision-making track that focuses on building your own productivity, turn to Chapter 2, Maximizing Your Own Productivity, page 11.

CHAPTER 56

Helping People Better Evaluate Their Activity to Improve Learning

Drawing from Covey's simple three-step cycle of organizing, acting, and evaluating, you launch a companywide campaign to get everyone more actively evaluating their work on a daily and weekly basis to ensure that they're working based on principles, not procedures, and always focusing on first things first. To help employees better evaluate, you use the following questions from Covey's book *First Things First:*

- Which goals did I achieve?
- What empowered me to accomplish these goals?
- What challenges did I encounter?
- How did I overcome them?
- Was accomplishing these goals the best use of my time?
- Did my focus on these goals blind me to unexpected opportunities for better use of my time?
- Did meeting these goals add to my personal integrity account?
- Which goals did I not achieve?
- What kept me from accomplishing these goals?

- As a result of the choices I made, did I use my time in better ways than I had planned?
- Did my choices make deposits or withdrawals from my personal integrity account?
- What unmet goals should I carry into the coming week?
- Did I take time for renewal, reflection, and recommitment?
- Did I take time to sharpen the saw on a daily basis?
- How did the time spent in renewal impact other areas?
- In what ways was I able to create synergy between roles and goals?
- How was I able to apply character and competence gained in one role to other roles?
- What principles did I apply or fail to apply during the week and what was the effect?
- What can I learn from the week as a whole?

With these questions printed and passed around in various forms throughout the divisions of FaraCom, you see a new enthusiasm for evaluating work. One of your division presidents, Lisa Harshaw, recommends publishing a journal that facilitates evaluation on a daily, weekly, and monthly basis. She comments, "Since using this simple 'organize, act, and evaluate' cycle, I realize how much I can learn from monitoring my activities. In fact, monitoring the past and present has become much more important for me than planning the future because when I monitor effectively, I can automatically reposition myself for the future. We started using a journal that we printed for every employee that makes it easier to use the three-step monitoring cycle. Everyone loves it."

You take Lisa up on her proposal to print an evaluation journal. After using the first 2,000 copies internally, you authorize publication of the book, which sells 60,000 copies in its first three months on the market. By the end of the year, FaraCom's sales increase to $1.2 billion, with profits climbing to $154 million, as shown in the following:

Selected Financial and Productivity Information
(Revenues and Profits in $ Millions)

	Fifth Year	Fourth Year
Revenues	$1,228	$1,009
Profits	154	131
Employees	2,565	1,943
Revenues per Employee (Actual $)	$478,752	$519,300
Profits per Employee (Actual $)	$60,039	$67,422

As you look back over your five years as CEO of FaraCom, you're glad you took an organizationwide view of productivity and that you used the Covey Leadership Organization to build productivity in the lives of every employee. Now the future looks brighter than ever.

This concludes your decision making on this track, but you can continue playing *The Productivity Game* by selecting one of the options below.

If you would like to see how this outcome stacks up against the other outcomes in the game, turn to Chapter 61, page 221.

If you want to review the other choices you could have made at your last decision-making point, turn to Chapters 55 and 57, pages 201 and 209.

To pursue another decision-making track that deals with building productivity companywide, turn to Chapter 13, Installing EmpowerTech's Improvement System, page 61.

To embark on a totally different decision-making track that focuses on building your own productivity, turn to Chapter 2, Maximizing Your Own Productivity, page 11.

CHAPTER 57

Building Win-Win Stewardship Agreements

Once again, you draw on Covey's *First Things First* and the Covey Leadership Organization to help you build win-win stewardship agreements throughout the company. According to Covey, "The stewardship agreement is a marked departure from traditional delegation, which often degenerates into 'dumping' tasks on others. The stewardship agreement creates synergistic partnerships among people to accomplish first things first together. Delegation becomes stewardship delegation. Instead of feeling 'dumped on,' people are involved. They're motivated. Both parties are accomplishing things of shared importance."

You ask your division presidents to embrace this philosophy and use it to take FaraCom to the next level of productivity. However, Mona Sork, president of retail operations, expresses a major concern, "Don't you think we need something with a more hands-on, practical orientation? This feels vague and fuzzy to me." When your other division presidents agree, you immediately launch into a discussion of the importance of stewardship as an important new management technique that fosters ownership, shared vision, and mutual respect. After further discussion, your seven division presidents agree to move forward with the stewardship agreements, but you sense a lack of deep commitment to the program. You immediately begin implementing the five elements of a win-win stewardship agreement:

1. Specify desired results.

2. Set guidelines.

3. Identify available resources.

4. Define accountability.

5. Determine the consequences.

You ask every employee throughout FaraCom to embrace these five elements and use them in every interaction with a subordinate, a team member, or a superior. You tell employees throughout the company to talk back to their bosses, asking for win-win stewardship agreements.

Over the next few months you continue to receive feedback that your division presidents do not support your idea of win-win stewardship agreements wholeheartedly. You respond to this feedback by asking employees to demand win-win stewardship agreements with their bosses, which begins to develop a chasm between you and your division presidents. In one case, a Greg Martin, a sales manager in the magazine publishing division, showed up on Alan Peay's doorstep at 10:30 P.M. to demand a win-win stewardship discussion. When Martin refused to leave, Peay called 911. The police dragged Martin away as he accused Peay of being a liar. The next day the story spread through FaraCom's seven divisions like wildfire, further infuriating the division presidents.

By the beginning of the fourth quarter of your fifth year as CEO, the alienation between you and your division presidents has reached crisis proportions. Employees throughout the organization at lower levels appreciate your openness and commitment to win-win stewardship agreements but accuse your seven division presidents and their management teams of failing to live up to the principles involved. More confrontations, similar to but less dramatic than the Peay-Martin experience, erupt between each division's management and subordinates.

Over the next few weeks, much of the progress made in living by principles and stressing first things first comes to a screeching halt, even backsliding, as people everywhere speak of the hypocrisy in FaraCom's senior management. You make the mistake of publicly criticizing your seven division presidents, which removes any possibility of reconciling with them in the short term—a problem Bill Faragut considers unresolvable without your resignation. In a confidential interview he says, "I can't fire all seven division presidents, so I'm firing you."

As you look back at your almost five years at FaraCom, you cringe at the harsh lesson you've learned: Practical guidelines must always follow conceptual ideas. You now realize that the conceptual win-win stewardship agreements needed more practical guidelines, tips, and examples than you provided.

This marks the end of your decision making on this track, but you can continue playing *The Productivity Game* by selecting one of the options below.

If you want to see how this outcome compares with other possibilities, turn to Chapter 61, page 221.

If you would like to see how the other two choices from your last decision would have worked out, turn to Chapters 55 and 56, pages 201 and 205.

If you want to pursue another decision-making path that deals with building productivity in the entire organization, turn to Chapter 13, Installing EmpowerTech's Improvement System, page 61.

To try a totally different decision-making track that focuses on your own productivity, turn to Chapter 2, Maximizing Your Own Productivity, page 11.

CHAPTER 58

Splitting Out FaraNet

Disappointed by Bill Faragut's negative reaction to your recommendation for splitting out FaraNet as the best way to maximize its growth, you turn up the pressure. Unfortunately, whether because of pride or stubbornness, Bill Faragut tells you that he will do whatever it takes to stop you from splitting out FaraNet.

Over the next few weeks you work around the clock with Wall Street lawyers and investment bankers to put a deal together that will allow you to take FaraNet out of FaraCom in a way that Bill Faragut can't refuse. With all your ducks in order, you once again approach Bill with an offer for FaraCom to remain a 40 percent owner of FaraNet in an initial public offering that would raise $300 million for future growth and expansion. You tell Faragut that if he does not accept this offer, you will leave FaraCom to establish another communications network, causing him to miss out on owning 40 percent of what will become, you're convinced, the fastest growing company in U.S. history.

To strengthen your case, you draw on some of the most reputable analysts and investment bankers in the industry to describe, in detail, the full extent of the opportunity available to FaraNet. Luckily, other members of the board help soften Bill Faragut, convincing him to support the split-out of FaraNet under your leadership. When he finally agrees, you quickly put into motion the legal documentation, due diligence, and public offering materials, with the help of a small army of Wall Street advisers, in order to initiate the public offering by May of your fifth year as CEO of FaraCom. In late April, while remaining CEO of FaraCom, you also assume the post of chairman and CEO of FaraNet, where you become a 15 percent shareholder as part of the public offering.

By the middle of June, FaraNet has raised over $300 million in equity funds to accommodate future growth and development of the $100 million company. In the second half of the year, you improve access to FaraNet by instituting a new system of ID numbers and passwords that make linking up with the network as easy as picking up the phone. FaraNet also develops new quick-view navigation software that allows users and other cruisers on the Internet to find products in seconds by using command words relating to topics, subjects, authors, content, phrases, and a host of other easy-to-use access words. Revenues quadruple to $400 million by the end of your fifth year as CEO of FaraCom and your first year as chairman and CEO of FaraNet. FaraCom sales also grow to $1.7 billion, with profits of $256 million, as shown below:

Selected Financial and Productivity Information
(Revenues and Profits in $ Millions)

	Fifth Year	Fourth Year
Revenues	$1,741*	$1,338
Profits	256*	199
Employees	3,281	2,978
Revenues per Employee (Actual $)	$530,631	$449,295
Profits per Employee (Actual $)	$78,025	$66,823

*Includes 40% of FaraNet revenues and profits.

With a projection that FaraNet will surpass $1 billion in the coming year, Bill Faragut has become your greatest fan and adds the title of Chairman of FaraCom to your others. As Bill Faragut steps down, you reflect on your five years as CEO of FaraCom and your bright future as chairman and CEO of both companies, although you expect to make Pete Rozinsky CEO of FaraNet within the year. Your reflection causes you to conclude that technology provides the ultimate key to productivity improvement. As you embark on the new year, the American Business Press dubs you the "King of the Internet" and proclaims you the first recognized national leader of the information superhighway revolution.

This marks the end of a very successful decision-making track, but you can still continue playing *The Productivity Game* by selecting one of the options below.

If you would like to see how this outcome stacks up with other outcomes in the game, turn to Chapter 61, page 221.

If you want to see how the other choices from your last decision-making point turned out, turn to Chapters 59 and 60, pages 217 and 219.

To pursue another decision-making track that also deals with building productivity companywide, turn to Chapter 11, Adopting Franklin's Time Management Program, page 53.

To embark on a totally different decision-making track that focuses on building your own productivity, turn to Chapter 2, Maximizing Your Own Productivity, page 11.

CHAPTER 59

Remaining Integrated as a Single Company

Knowing that Bill Faragut would oppose any splitting out of FaraNet and feeling concerned that a merger with QVC could hinder FaraCom's growth and development, you take the path of least resistance, hoping that you'll not regret it. However, during the first few months of your fifth year as CEO of FaraCom, the pressure for building all eight divisions, particularly FaraNet, become unbearable. You're torn in so many directions that FaraNet languishes without the necessary funding for growth and the clear management mandate to exploit its unique opportunity. By mid-year, you see Genie, General Electric's network, attempting to supplant FaraNet as the leading communications and entertainment network, which causes you to reverse your position and plead with Bill Faragut to split out FaraNet as soon as possible. Not surprisingly, Bill Faragut has not changed his mind and wants nothing to do with a split-out or a merger.

Out of sheer frustration, you resign as president and CEO of FaraCom. And while Bill Faragut tries to get you to change your mind, you remain as stubborn as he, telling him that he'll be sorry for the decision not to split out FaraNet. Knowing that you've burned bridges impulsively before, you hope the fallout from this one will prove positive for you in the future. You immediately begin discussing job opportunities with General Electric, U.S. West, IBM, and Novell, as well as considering the possibility of establishing your own network through a start-up venture funded by Merrill Lynch.

While your future looks bright in the arena of communications networks and the worldwide Internet, your decision making at FaraCom comes to an abrupt halt. However, you can continue playing the game by selecting one of the options below.

To see how this outcome compares with other possibilities in The Productivity Game, *turn to Chapter 61, page 221.*

If you want to see how the other two choices from your last decision turned out, turn to Chapters 58 and 60, pages 213 and 219.

To pursue another decision-making track that deals with building productivity companywide, turn to Chapter 11, Adopting Franklin's Time Management Program, page 53.

To embark on a totally different decision-making track that focuses on building your own productivity, turn to Chapter 2, Maximizing Your Own Productivity, page 11.

CHAPTER 60

Merging with QVC

Deciding that Bill Faragut will never agree to a merger with QVC, you devise an alternative strategy with QVC executives that leads you to resign as CEO of FaraCom and accept a position at QVC as president of network services, hoping it will force Faragut into a merger with QVC. The move so startles Bill Faragut that he pleads with you to return. When you refuse, he reluctantly enters into merger negotiations with QVC management. However, after weeks of negotiating, the talks fall apart as Bill Faragut holds on to his position of maintaining independence for certain FaraCom divisions. He also communicates to a *Wall Street Journal* reporter, "In the final analysis, I guess I decided not to do the deal because of mistrust. The way this thing was handled from the beginning has been sneaky." Sadly, you wonder whether some other course might not have accomplished the QVC merger. To make matters worse, QVC management informs you that without FaraCom and FaraNet your position with the company seems tenuous.

After discussing the matter with several executives, you finally conclude that QVC also has a trust problem, even though they'd never admit it. So many questions have been raised about the way in which you left FaraCom and your inability to make a merger happen that you finally conclude that your reputation within QVC will not allow you to succeed. You accept an attractive severance package from QVC and begin your search for a company that needs a CEO.

This marks the end of your decision making on this track, but you can continue playing *The Productivity Game* by selecting one of the options below.

To see how this outcome compares with other possibilities in the game, turn to Chapter 61, page 221.

If you want to see how the other two choices in your last decision turned out, turn to Chapters 58 and 59, pages 213 and 217.

To try another decision-making track that deals with building productivity companywide, turn to Chapter 11, Adopting Franklin's Time Management Program, page 53.

To embark on a totally different decision-making path that focuses on building your own productivity, turn to Chapter 2, Maximizing Your Own Productivity, page 11.

CHAPTER 61

A Ranking of the Outcome

Caution: Your experience playing *The Productivity Game* will be enhanced if you wait to read this chapter until after you have come to the end of a decision-making track.

Your experience to this point should have enhanced your productivity insight and decision-making ability. In developing this game, I intended more than anything else to broaden, deepen, and strengthen your productivity consciousness and competence. I also hope playing *The Productivity Game* has entertained and inspired you through its virtual reality challenges, dilemmas, and choices.

There are 27 outcomes in the game, ranging from triumph to disaster. In order to compare the various outcomes, find the number of the chapter you just completed (which represents the end of a decision-making track) ranked on the following page according to profits per employee at the end of five years or according to the reason for your departure prior to completing five years as CEO. All outcomes, both positive and negative, are ranked, but only those that allowed you to complete five years as CEO show revenues and profits per employee.

Ending Chapter	Profits per Employee	Revenues per Employee	Revenues*	Profits*
58	$78,025	$530,631	$1,741	$256
47	$74,610	$521,158	$1,404	$201
55	$66,799	$520,080	$1,308	$168
51	$61,649	$518,052	$1,521	$181
34	$60,081	$477,796	$2,012	$253
56	$60,039	$478,752	$1,228	$154
50	$58,135	$513,070	$1,315	$149
48	$52,448	$503,497	$1,152	$120
38	$40,043	$501,082	$1,389	$111
49	$37,582	$447,712	$1,096	$92
54	$36,728	$396,077	$949	$88
44	$26,572	$389,725	$880	$60
42	$17,343	$381,980	$903	$41

*Revenues and Profits in $ Millions

Ending Chapter	Reason for Departure
35	You leave for Viacom-Paramount
36	You leave for Ernst & Young
60	You leave for QVC
45	You leave for a small consulting firm
46	You decide to step down as CEO
37	FaraCom is sold
59	You resign
53	You resign
39	Faragut asks for your resignation
43	Faragut asks for your resignation
41	You're fired
52	You're fired
40	You're fired
57	You're fired

Now that you know how your initial choices in *The Productivity Game* stack up, put your productivity consciousness and competence to the test again by choosing one of the options at the end of the chapter you just finished. When you reach the end of another decision-making track, you can return to this chapter to compare your results. Good luck.

Bibliography
Sources Referred to
in *The Productivity Game*

Bridges, William, "The End of the Job," *Fortune,* Vol. 130, No. 6, September 19, 1994, pp. 62–74.

Champy, James, *Reengineering Management.* New York: Harper Business, 1995.

Covey, Stephen, Roger Merrill, and Rebecca Merrill, *First Things First.* New York: Simon & Schuster, 1994.

Covey, Stephen, *The Seven Habits of Highly Effective People.* New York: Simon & Schuster, 1989.

de Bono, Edward, *Six Thinking Hats.* Boston: Little, Brown & Company, 1985.

Emerson, Ralph Waldo, "The Poet," *Ralph Waldo Emerson: A Critical Edition of the Major Works.* Oxford: Oxford University Press, 1990.

Fisher, Anne, "Welcome to the Age of Overwork," *Fortune,* Vol. 126, No. 13, November 30, 1992, pp. 64-71.

Fox, Matthew, *The Reinvention of Work.* New York: HarperCollins, 1994.

Goldratt, Eliyahu and Jeff Cox, *The Goal: A Process of Ongoing Improvement.* Great Barrington, MA: The North River Press, 1984.

———, *It's Not Luck.* Great Barrington, MA: The North River Press, 1994.

Grove, Andrew, *High Output Management.* New York: Random House, 1983.

Hamel, Gary and C. K. Prahalad, *The Competitive Future*. Boston: Harvard Business School Press, 1994.

Hickman, Craig, Craig Bott, Marlon Berrett, and Brad Angus, *The Fourth Dimension*. New York: John Wiley & Sons, 1995.

Keirsey, David and Marilyn Bates, *Please Understand Me: Character and Temperament Types*. New York: Prometheus Nemesis Book Company, 1984.

Naisbitt, John, *Global Paradox*. New York: William Morrow & Company, 1994.

Nonaka, Ikujiro, "The Knowledge Creating Company," *Harvard Business Review*, Vol. 69, No. 6, 1992, pp. 96–104.

Schatz, Ken, *Managing by Influence*. New York: John Wiley & Sons, 1990.

Scherer, John and Larry Shook, *Work and the Human Spirit*. Spokane, WA: John Scherer & Associates, 1993.

Schlesinger, Len, *The Real Heroes of Business and Not a CEO Among Them*. New York: Currency Doubleday, 1993.

Schor, Juliet, *The Overworked American*. New York: Basic Books, 1991.

Sibson, Robert, *Maximizing Employee Productivity*. New York: Amacom, 1994.

Smith, Hyrum, *Ten Natural Laws of Time and Life Management*. New York: Warner Books, 1994.

Weisbord, Marvin, *Productive Workplaces*. San Francisco, Jossey-Bass, 1987.

Wikström, Solveig and Richard Norman, *Knowledge and Value*. London: Routledge, 1994.